NELSON

ARTS

GOING THE DISTANCE

Gerald Best

Caren Cameron

Maureen Dockendorf

Barb Eklund

Christine Finochio

Ruth Hay

Sharon Jeroski

Eugene Mazur

Mary McCarthy

Maureen Skinner

Senior Program Consultant

Jennette MacKenzie

I(T)P Nelson

an International Thomson Publishing company

Toronto • Albany • Bonn • Boston • Cincinnati • Detroit • London • Madrid • Melbourne
Mexico City • New York • Pacific Grove • Paris • San Francisco • Singapore • Tokyo • Washington

Grade 6 Reviewers:

Judy Butler
Sydney, Nova Scotia

Jackie Copp
Winnipeg, Manitoba

Diana Cruise
Winnipeg, Manitoba

Karen Curry
Amherst, Nova Scotia

Carol Germyn
Calgary, Alberta

Jane Mills
Burnaby, British Columbia

Craig Parrott
Essex, Ontario

Ann Louise Revells
Nepean, Ontario

Shirley Sturdevant
Chatham, Ontario

Catherine Walker
Edmonton, Alberta

Jan Wells
Vancouver, British Columbia

Equity Consultant:
Ken Ramphal

I(T)P® International Thomson Publishing
The ITP logo is a trademark under licence
www.thomson.com

Published by
I(T)P®Nelson
A division of Thomson Canada Limited, 1998
1120 Birchmount Road
Scarborough, Ontario M1K 5G4
www.nelson.com

Printed and bound in Canada

1 2 3 4 5 6 7 8 9 0 / ML/ 7 6 5 4 3 2 1 0 9 8

Canadian Cataloguing in Publication Data

Main entry under title:

Nelson language arts 6

ISBN 0-17-607527-5 (v. 1 : bound)
ISBN 0-17-607446-5 (v. 1 : pbk.)
Contents: [1] Going the Distance

1. Readers (Elementary). I. Cameron, Caren, 1949–

PE1121.N448 1998   428.6   C97-931515-8

Project Team: Angela Cluer, Mark Cobham, Kathleen ffolliott, Vicki Gould, Susan Green, Ann Ludbrook, John McInnes, Marcia Miron, David Spiegel, Theresa Thomas

Art Direction and Production: Liz Harasymczuk

TABLE OF CONTENTS

Unit 1 *Going the Distance* 6

Unit 2 *Searching for Evidence*   78

Unit 3 *Media Messages* 136

Unit 1: *Going the Distance*

What are some things you have achieved in your life? Have you thought about personal goals you would like to attain? In this unit, you will read stories and poems about characters who have set goals, met personal challenges, and tried to achieve their "personal best." As you read and talk about their personal goals and plans you will explore your own thoughts, feelings, and experiences and learn more about yourself. You will

- read stories and poems about setting goals and striving for "personal best"
- use language to explore thoughts, ideas, feelings, and experiences
- think and talk about your own experiences
- learn to use charts to organize your ideas
- learn some tips to help you become a better reader
- develop a plan to achieve a personal goal

It's Easy to Dream

Written by Zaro Weil

It's easy to dream
Just wait for
Evening
To powder the sky
With a million thoughts

And then
Select a few for yourself.

Dream Chasers

Written by Susan Hughes
Illustrated by Farida Zaman

READING TIP

Think about your experiences

Often we dream about things we would like to do or what we would like to be in the future. Think about something you have dreamed about accomplishing. What could you do to make it happen?

What are the things you dream about? Do you imagine becoming a great chess player or shooting a goal in the final game of the season? Do you think about making it onto the cross-country team or writing a perfect poem? Maybe you want to find a best friend or work at turning a good friendship into an even better one!

It's fun to dream. And it's important to dream. By reflecting on our dreams, we can learn about ourselves. We can learn what matters to us.

Some dreams come, some dreams go. But when a dream lasts, it opens our eyes. A dream that continues to spark our imagination is special. It could be the one that springs us into action.

Into action? Sure. After all, we can reach out and try to touch our dreams.

Here's proof. Read about these young Canadians who have chased their dreams. Yes, they have had to give up some other things. They have had to focus and be persistent. But they have had fun and are proud of themselves. These ordinary kids have combined dreaming with hard work—and done some exceptional things!

Carlee and Christy Panylyk

Entrepreneurs (Hinton, Alberta)

★ ★ ★

It all began in 1994 when nine-year-old Carlee Panylyk wanted some extra summer money. She had a brain wave. All summer long, Carlee made and sold marble bags to her friends. She also began making shoe bags and swim bags. She sold them at farmers' markets and craft shows. The bags were a hit! They were also a lot of work to make.

So the next summer, Carlee asked her seven-year-old sister, Christy, to be her business partner. They spent about two hours a day all summer making Re-Cyc-A-Bags—cloth bags that would hold plastic bags for recycling.

The two sisters have never looked back. In 1995, they formed their own business, Carlee and Christy's Creations. They now sell very popular pewter necklaces. As of now, their company has earned more than $50,000.

"At the start, I was extremely nervous. I was worried I might not do well. I was also nervous talking to customers," says Christy.

But as people scooped up the items and Christy gained more experience, her fears vanished. "I feel a lot more confident talking to people now. And I've learned a lot. I know that it takes a plan, time, and energy to make a successful business work."

To other aspiring young entrepreneurs, Carlee suggests: "Have confidence in yourself and don't give up!" ★

Heather Kao

Musician (St. John's, Newfoundland)

★ ★ ★

"Ever since I could talk, I would ask for the violin. Ever since I could walk, I would reach for it," explains Heather Kao.

When she was four, her parents finally gave her a violin. She loved practising every day and never needed to be reminded. When she was 12, Heather's father suggested that she try out for the National Youth Orchestra. Wow! thought Heather. She knew that the National Youth Orchestra accepts only the best young performers from across Canada. Performers are between 14 and 28 years of age and must audition for a spot every year. The orchestra members train together for several weeks in July and then perform on tour for the rest of the summer.

After hours and hours of practising, Heather did her first audition tape for the NYO. Even though she knew she was too young to be accepted, she was still really nervous.

"It was pretty scary," Heather remembers. "But going through the audition process was a great learning experience."

The next year, she auditioned again and was accepted into the orchestra—as the youngest member! In 1994, she travelled with the NYO across Canada. In 1996, she travelled with the NYO to Japan.

"It was very intimidating at first, because I was so young. But everyone was warm and friendly," says Heather. "We were like a big family by the end. It was wonderful to have a chance to play with a really great orchestra!" ★

Amaan Merali

Artist (Toronto, Ontario)

★ ★ ★

Amaan Merali has been interested in art since he was two years old. He doodled all the time, but his work never moved beyond cartoon characters.

Then in grade seven, Amaan became immediately intrigued by the different techniques introduced by his art teacher. "I wanted to know more about everything," he says.

Once Amaan's interest was sparked, he has never looked back. He has worked hard to become the best artist he can be. And that is pretty amazingly good! His art has been described as fantastic and sophisticated.

"I sketch all the time. I complete two or three drawings a week. I am committed to my art," says Amaan. "Every week, I can see my work improving. I know that I'm going to keep getting better."

Amaan works with chalk, feather and ink, gouache, pencil, charcoal, and even oil paints. Amaan paints portraits,

some large and some small. Many are of his friends, and some he sells. Amaan was one of 120 promising young art students chosen to participate in a week-long residential arts camp run by his board of education in the fall of 1997.

Amaan gets a lot of support from his parents and his friends.

"I listen to people's comments about my work, and sometimes I change what I have done. I just keep on practising," he emphasizes. ★

13

Jeremy Olson

Magician (Coquitlam, British Columbia)

★ ★ ★

Jeremy is 10 years old—and has already been a magician for five years!

He remembers the day he got hooked on magic. A magician in a local store pulled a coin out of his ear. Jeremy immediately wanted to learn how to do tricks, too.

"At first, the tricks that I was doing weren't that great. As I got better, the tricks got more interesting. As I improved, it was easier for me to do harder tricks," says Jeremy.

Jeremy works hard learning the craft of magic. Every day, he practises tricks for anywhere from half an hour to three hours.

All his practice has been paying off. Jeremy has been a member of the Vancouver Magic Circle since he was eight. (No one younger has ever been admitted.) He has won many first-place honours in magic competitions. In 1997, he was a finalist for a YTV Achievement Award.

Jeremy is devoted to the art of magic. "He has a natural ability," says his mother. "Plus he is centred and focused. That's why he does so well."

"I practise a trick a lot when I am going to perform it. Then I show it. I'm not nervous, because I know I've practised a lot. I know it will go all right," says Jeremy. ★

Georgetown Environmental Club (Grades 5 to 8)

Environmentalism (Georgetown, P.E.I.)

★ ★ ★

The Georgetown Environmental Club has been around for years. It is made up of 25 to 30 dedicated students from grades 5 to 8 at Georgetown Elementary School. New kids join every year and become keen on doing their bit to help their local environment.

"These kids are itching to take part and get involved," says the school's principal, Kevin Stonefield. And that's despite having to write an essay and be interviewed before being accepted into the Club!

Jennifer Gotell, 12, has been in the Club for two years. "I joined because I enjoy the outdoors," she says. "I want to make a difference."

And that's exactly what the Club is all about. They've been cleaning the beach, planting trees at an old unused dump, and generally cleaning up around town every year. They worked for several years to clean up garbage and debris from a watershed area surrounding local Teddy's Dam. They also built nesting boxes for birds, planted seedlings, and built a nature trail in the area. For this, the Georgetown Environmental Club won the top National Wildlife Week award in 1996.

"Sometimes I get a bit discouraged. But I remember the reason I started doing this," says Jennifer. "I don't really consider it work. I enjoy it!" ★

Iris Bonaise

Public Service (Little Pine First Nation, Cut Knife, Saskatchewan)

★ ★ ★

It all really started with Denis Joseph. That was Iris Bonaise's brother. He died of cancer in 1994. One evening in January, 1997, Iris was looking at photographs of her brother.

"My gears started turning," Iris remembers. She suddenly felt she had to raise some money for cancer research and raise some awareness about the disease that had ended her brother's life.

A bake sale didn't seem ambitious enough.

"Why don't I walk to Saskatoon?" Iris remembers asking her father. That is where her brother lived and died. It is also a long way from Iris's home—175 kilometres, in fact!

Iris trained for months. She walked farther and farther every week. With her father, she planned her route. Then on September 13 she set out on her Walk for Cancer.

"I was determined that I was going to get to my finishing point," Iris says. "I knew I could do it."

And four days later she did, raising donations for cancer research along the way. The elders wanted to recognize the importance of Iris's walk. In a special ceremony, they "smudged" Iris. They burned sweetgrass and rubbed the smoke on her.

"I felt proud of myself," Iris says. "I didn't know I would make that big of an impression!" ★

You've heard it before: Do your best.

It's easy to say it. But think about it for a moment. It's not so easy to do your best. Especially if it means giving up things or doing things that might be a bit scary. Especially if it means working hard, practising, and training—over and over, again and again.

Iris Bonaise did it. Jeremy Olson is still doing it. But they aren't the only ones. There are kids all around you doing their best. Maybe you are too. And there is something wonderful about doing your best and chasing your dream, whether or not you catch it.

Let's leave the last words to Heather Kao. She says, "You are good in your own way. Believe in yourself because that will get you everywhere you want to go."

★ ★ ★

AFTER YOU READ

Think about what you've learned

Make a list of some of the things you've learned about achieving a personal goal. Review your list and develop criteria for setting goals and achieving them. Why do you think the author chose these young Canadians to be interviewed for this selection? How do they meet your goal-setting and goal-achieving criteria?

The Night of the Pomegranate

Written by Tim Wynne-Jones
Illustrated by Tadeusz Majewski

READING TIP

Make a personal response

As you read, pause after each page and think about your ideas, feelings, images, and opinions. Record your responses in a chart like the one here.

Ideas	Images
Feelings	Opinions

Harriet's solar system was a mess. She had made it—the sun and its nine planets—out of rolled-up balls of the morning newspaper. It was mounted on a sheet of green Bristol board. The Bristol board had a project about Austria on the other side. Harriet wished the background were black. Green was all wrong.

Everything about her project was wrong. The crumpled paper was coming undone. Because she had used the last of the Scotch tape on Saturn's rings, the three remaining planets had nothing to keep them scrunched up. Tiny Pluto was already bigger than Jupiter and growing by the minute. She had also run out of glue, so part of her solar system was stuck together with grape chewing gum.

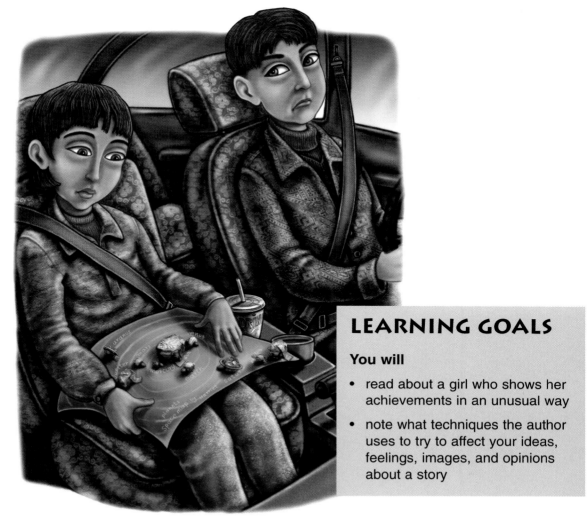

LEARNING GOALS

You will

- read about a girl who shows her achievements in an unusual way

- note what techniques the author uses to try to affect your ideas, feelings, images, and opinions about a story

Harriet's big brother, Tom, was annoyed at her because Mom made him drive her to school early with her stupid project. Dad was annoyed at her for using part of the business section. Mostly she had stuck to the want ads, but then an advertisement printed in red ink in the business section caught her eye, and she just had to have it for Mars. Harriet had a crush on Mars; that's what Tom said. She didn't even mind him saying it.

Mars was near the Earth this month. The nights had been November cold but clear as glass, and Harriet had been out to see Mars every night, which was why she hadn't got her solar system finished, why she was so tired, why Mom made Tom drive her to school. It was all Mars's fault.

She was using the tape on Ms. Krensky's desk when Clayton Beemer arrived with his dad. His solar system came from the hobby store. The planets were Styrofoam balls, all different sizes and painted the right colours. Saturn's rings were clear plastic painted over as delicately as insect wings.

Harriet looked at her own Saturn. Her rings were drooping despite all the tape. They looked like a limp skirt on a ... on a ball of scrunched-up newspaper.

Harriet sighed. The wires that supported Clayton's planets in their black box were almost invisible. The planets seemed to float.

"What d'ya think?" Clayton asked. He beamed. Mr. Beemer beamed. Harriet guessed that *he* had made the black box with its glittery smears of stars.

She had rolled up her own project protectively when Clayton entered the classroom. Suddenly one of the planets came unstuck and fell on the floor. Clayton and Mr. Beemer looked at it.

"What's that?" asked Clayton.

"Pluto, I think," said Harriet, picking it up. She popped it in her mouth. It tasted of grape gum. "Yes, Pluto," she said. Clayton and Mr. Beemer walked away to find the best place to show off their project.

Darjit arrived next. "Hi, Harriet," she said. The project under her arm had the planets' names done in bold gold lettering. Harriet's heart sank. Pluto tasted stale and cold.

But last night Harriet had tasted pomegranates. Old Mrs. Pond had given her one while she busied herself putting on layer after layer of warm clothing and gathering the things they would need for their Mars watch.

Mrs. Pond lived in the country. She lived on the edge of the woods by a meadow that sloped down to a marsh through rough frost-licked grass and prickly ash and juniper. It was so much darker than town; good for star-gazing.

By eleven p.m., Mars was directly above the marsh, which was where Harriet and Mrs. Pond set themselves up for their vigil. They found it just where they had left it the night before: in the constellation Taurus between the Pleiades and the Hyades. But you didn't need a map to find Mars these nights. It shone like rust, neither trembling nor twinkling as the fragile stars did.

Mrs. Pond smiled and handed Harriet two folded-up golfers' chairs. "Ready?" she asked.

"Ready, class?" said Ms. Krensky. Everyone took their seats. Harriet placed the green Bristol board universe in front of her. It was an even worse mess than it had been when she arrived. Her solar system was ravaged.

It had started off with Pluto and then, as a joke to make Darjit laugh, she had eaten Neptune. Then Karen had come in, and Jodi and Nick and Scott.

"The planet taste test," Harriet had said, ripping off a bit of Mercury. "Umm, very spicy." By the time the bell rang there wasn't much of her project left.

Kevin started. He stood at the back of the classroom holding a green and blue marble.

"If this was Earth," he said, "then the sun would be this big—." He put the Earth in his pocket and then pulled a fat squishy yellow beach ball from a garbage bag. Everybody hooted and clapped. "And it would be at the crosswalk," he added. Everyone looked confused, so Ms. Krensky helped Kevin explain the relative distances between the Earth and the sun. "And Pluto would be eighty kilometres away from here," said Kevin. But then he wasn't sure about that, so Ms. Krensky worked it out at the board with him.

Meanwhile, using Kevin's example, the class was supposed to figure out where other planets in the solar system would be relative to the green and blue marble in Kevin's pocket. Harriet sighed.

Until last night, Harriet had never seen the inside of a pomegranate before. As she opened the hard rind, she

marvelled at the bright red seeds in their cream-coloured fleshy pouches.

"It's like a little secret universe all folded in on itself," said Mrs. Pond.

Harriet tasted it. With her tongue, she popped a little red bud against the roof of her mouth. The taste startled her, made her laugh.

"Tonight," Mrs. Pond said, "Mars is only 77 million kilometres away." They drank a cocoa toast to that. Then she told Harriet about another time when Mars had been even closer on its orbit around the sun. She had been a girl then, and had heard on the radio the famous broadcast of "The War of the Worlds." An actor named Orson Welles had made a radio drama based on a story about Martians attacking the world, but he had made it in a series of news bulletins and reports, and a lot of people had believed it was true.

Harriet listened to Mrs. Pond and sipped her cocoa and stared at the Earth's closest neighbour and felt deliciously chilly and warm at the same time. Mars was wonderfully clear in the telescope, but even with the naked eye she could imagine canals and raging storms. She knew there weren't really

Martians, but she allowed herself to imagine them anyway. She imagined one of them preparing for his invasion of the Earth, packing his laser gun, a thermos of cocoa, and a golfer's chair.

"What in heaven's name is this?" Ms. Krensky was standing at Harriet's chair staring down at the green Bristol board. There was only one planet left.

"Harriet says it's Mars." Darjit started giggling.

"And how big is Mars?" asked Ms. Krensky. Her eyes said Unsatisfactory.

"Compared to Kevin's marble Earth, Mars would be the size of a pomegranate seed, including the juicy red pulp," said Harriet. Ms. Krensky walked to the front of the class. She turned at her desk. Was there the hint of a smile on her face?

"And where is it?" she asked, raising an eyebrow.

Harriet looked at the calculations she had done on a corner of the green Bristol board. "If the sun was at the crosswalk," said Harriet, "then Mars would be much closer. Over there." She pointed out the window at the slide in the kindergarten playground. Some of the class actually looked out the window to see if they could see it.

"You *can* see Mars," said Harriet. "Sometimes." Now she was sure she saw Ms. Krensky smile.

"How many of you have seen Mars?" the teacher asked. Only Harriet and Randy Pilcher put up their hands. But Randy had only seen it in a movie.

"Last night was a special night, I believe," said Ms. Krensky, crossing her arms and leaning against her desk. Harriet nodded. "Tell us about it, Harriet," said the teacher.

So Harriet did. She told them all about Mrs. Pond and the Mars watch. She started with the pomegranate.

AFTER YOU READ

Think about your responses

Review the information you recorded in your personal response chart. What parts of the story caused you to record the most ideas, the clearest images, and the strongest feelings and opinions? What did the author do to make you respond in this way?

The Great Eagle

Written by Jan Bourdeau Waboose
Excerpted from the book Morning on the Lake
Illustrated by Karen Reczuch

READING TIP

Identify with the character

Think of a time when you had to struggle against fear to achieve a goal. How did you try to overcome your fear? Read to see what the boy in this story did to overcome his fears and achieve his goals.

Grandfather is looking up. I know he is searching the sky. Grandfather is wise and knows many things. He says I will too.

"When, Mishomis?" I ask.

"In time," he answers. "Wisdom will come."

I stand beside Grandfather. I look up and search too. The sun is low on the horizon. I feel the wind's wings, warm on my arms and legs.

Grandfather speaks softly. "It is time—we will go."

I want to jump up and down and make a lot of noise. But I do not. For where we are going only silence is needed. We leave before the sun climbs to the centre of the sky.

I follow Grandfather like a shadow. Quietly, quickly, he moves like a fox, over the familiar path of the forest floor. I know that many animals have made this trail as they walked beneath the ancient white pines that whisper and past the singing water of the river.

But I don't see any of them today, only Grandfather ahead of me. I try to stay close behind, but it is not easy keeping up with his strong, silent strides. I stop a moment to taste a plump purple berry from a saskatoon bush and then hurry on.

I am hot and thirsty. There are beads of sweat on my nose. I am getting tired but I do not slow down.

Finally Grandfather stops. We are almost there. Almost. He turns to me and smiles. "You travel swiftly with soft steps. That is good. Now you must show strength as well."

He points to a rocky cliff and then tousles my hair with his long fingers. His dark brown eyes are bright and catch the sun's reflection.

"Are you ready, Noshen?"

I wipe the sweat from my nose, take a deep breath, and nod.

"I am, Mishomis."

Before we begin our climb, I watch my grandfather's strong brown arms reach out and spread open to the turquoise sky. So I too stretch my arms high. Grandfather looks at me and nods.

As I climb, I can feel each rough groove etched in the face of the cliff. Its surface is hot and dry under my sweaty palms. My fingers are red and tingling, and I feel the hard ridges of rock pressing against my bare knees.

The cliff is steep, so I avoid looking down. Although I am not afraid, I am tiring. I keep up with Grandfather, but my legs feel as heavy as rocks. I cannot let this slow me, for I know that many ancestors have climbed here before me, and before Grandfather too. I imagine each foothold, formed through time by their steps.

Finally, we reach the top. The sun is high. It is very still and quiet.

I can look back now, but as I turn, I notice a large shadow cast down on the ground. I quickly look up but cannot see what has made the shadow. Instead, I see thin birch trees waving in the soft breeze. It is strange because I cannot hear the leaves rustling. Neither can I feel the wind cooling my skin or smell the dry moss under my moccasins.

Up here, I stand closer to the noon sun, yet I do not feel the heat, nor do I have to shield my eyes from its brightness.

Grandfather sits down and motions for me to sit beside him. I do. He does not speak. Neither will I. This is his special place. Noon is his favourite time, and so it is mine.

We look out over the fast-flowing river and the thick green forest below. I can see with birds' eyes. I feel that I am soaring, touching the endless sky, floating through powder-white clouds. Flying free, high above our world.

Very still, we wait, perched on top of our rocky nest. I can hear my own breathing. It is loud. I cannot hear Grandfather's. I wonder if he is holding his breath. I want to look at him, take one quick peek. But then ... I see a powerful bird in slow motion. Alone and gliding.

In silence he moves with smooth graceful strokes.
Around and around, he circles us with wings reaching like
Mother's arms. Motionless, we watch.

The Great Eagle.

Suddenly, the eagle is looking at me. He is coming in
my direction. Faster and closer he flies.

I do not move, not one part of my body. Oh, how I
want to hold on to Grandfather. But I do not. My heart is
pounding like the beat of the drum.

And then the eagle swoops down. I can hear the rapid
rhythm of strong wings. I want to squeeze my eyes shut, but I
keep them open, watching. He is here. His scent fills my
nostrils. I feel talons combing through my hair with a
gentleness I cannot explain.

Then he is gone, as swiftly as he appeared.

I let out a long breath and look at Grandfather. He is

smiling, a very big smile. He points to the ground. There before us lies a long soft eagle feather.

I feel Grandfather's warm strong hands holding my shoulders as he speaks.

"Noshen, our people see the eagle as a powerful messenger. His presence is a sign of honour and wisdom. As the Great Eagle is a proud protector of our people, I am a proud Mishomis of my Noshen."

And so, I too am proud, just like Grandfather.

AFTER YOU READ

Make a character portrait

To make a character portrait, you describe someone using words instead of pictures. Write a character portrait of Noshen. Use words that describe his character and give examples from the story to support your description.

Cinder Edna

@

Written by Ellen Jackson
Illustrated by Kevin O'Malley

READING TIP

Make comparisons

How do you make the best of an unpleasant experience? What kind of attitude do you have when you face problems or things are not going the way you want them to? As you read, compare the thoughts and actions of the two characters to your own.

Once upon a time there were two girls who lived next door to each other. You may have heard of the first one. Her name was Cinderella. Poor Cinderella was forced to work from morning till night, cooking and scrubbing pots and pans and picking up after her cruel stepmother and wicked stepsisters. When her work was done, she sat among the cinders to keep warm, thinking about all her troubles.

Cinder Edna, the other girl, was also forced to work for her wicked stepmother and stepsisters. But she sang and whistled while she worked. Moreover, she had learned a thing or two from doing all that housework—such as how to make tuna casserole sixteen different ways and how to get spots off everything from rugs to ladybugs.

Edna had tried sitting in the cinders a few times. But it seemed like a silly way to spend time. Besides, it just made her clothes black and sooty. Instead when the housework was done, she kept warm by mowing the lawn and cleaning parrot cages for the neighbours at $1.50 an hour. She also taught herself to play the accordion.

Even with her ragged, sooty clothing Cinderella was quite beautiful.

Edna, on the other hand, wasn't much to look at. But she was strong and spunky and knew some good jokes— including an especially funny one about an anteater from Afghanistan.

Now, one day the king announced that he would give a ball and that all the ladies of the land were invited. Cinderella's stepsisters set about choosing what they would wear. All day they ordered Cinderella around as they made their preparations.

Cinder Edna's stepsisters were excited, too. On the evening of the ball they trimmed their toenails and flossed their teeth. They put on their most beautiful gowns and drove away, leaving Edna behind to clean up after them.

Cinderella sat among the cinders and sighed. "Oh how I wish I had a fairy godmother who could change these rags into a beautiful gown so that I, too, could go to the ball."

No sooner said than done. Cinderella *did* have a fairy godmother, and she just happened to be passing by. With a wave of her magic wand, she changed Cinderella's rags into a beautiful gown. On Cinderella's incredibly tiny feet appeared a pair of dainty glass slippers.

Cinder Edna didn't believe in fairy godmothers. Instead she had used her cage-cleaning money to put a dress on layaway for just these kinds of occasions.

"And my comfortable loafers will be perfect for dancing," she said as she slipped them onto her feet.

Meanwhile Cinderella's big, bright eyes brimmed with tears. "But, Fairy Godmother, how will I get to the ball?"

The fairy godmother was surprised that her goddaughter couldn't seem to figure anything out for herself. However, with another wave of the wand, she changed a pumpkin into a carriage, six white mice into horses, and a stray rat into a coachman.

"Be sure to leave before midnight," she warned Cinderella as she helped her into the elegant carriage.

Cinder Edna took the bus.

When Cinderella arrived at the ball, everyone thought she was a princess. The king's son Randolph was taken with her great beauty. He asked her to dance, but Cinderella could only sway a bit to the music. She was afraid of mussing her hair, and she knew those fragile glass slippers would break if she danced too hard.

Just then Cinder Edna entered the room. She made straight for the refreshment table and poured herself some punch. It was Randolph's princely duty to greet everyone, so he came over to say hello.

"What's it like, being a prince?" Edna asked, to make conversation.

"Quite fantastic," said the prince. "Mostly I review the troops and sit around on the throne looking brave and wise." He turned his head so that Edna could see how handsome his chin looked from the right side.

"Borrring," thought Edna.

"Excuse me, but we recycle plastic around here," said a little man with glasses and a warm smile.

"Just ignore him," said Randolph. "He's only my younger brother, Rupert. He lives in a cottage in the back and runs the recycling plant and a home for orphaned kittens."

Cinder Edna immediately handed Rupert her cup.

"Would you like to dance?" asked Rupert.

Cinder Edna and Rupert danced and danced. They did the Storybook Stomp and the Cinnamon Twist. They did the Worm and the Fish. They boogied and woogied. At last they stopped for a round of punch. Edna learned that Rupert (1) loved tuna casserole, (2) played the concertina, (3) knew some good jokes.

She told him the one about the anteater from Afghanistan and he told her the one about the banana from Barbados.

They were deep in a conversation about gum wrappers and rusty tin cans when the clock began to strike twelve.

"Oh," cried Cinderella, running for the door. "The magic spell disappears at midnight."

"Oh, oh," cried Cinder Edna, running for the door. "The buses stop running at midnight!"

Randolph and Rupert ran after the two girls.

"Wait! Wait!" they called. But it was too late.

As the girls vanished into the night, the two princes ran smack-dab into each other on the palace steps.

Whap! They landed with a thud. Rupert's glasses went flying and broke into a million pieces on the cement.

"Look what you made me do!" said Randolph. "Now she's gone—the only girl I ever loved."

"Well, didn't you get her name?" asked Rupert impatiently. "The one I love is named Edna."

"Gee, I forgot to ask," said Randolph, scratching his head.

As Rupert got up he stumbled over something. When he leaned close to look, he saw two shoes lying side by side on the steps. One was a scuffed-up loafer. The other was a dainty glass slipper. "These definitely should be recycled," he said.

"No! No!" said Randolph. "This is how we'll find them. We'll try these shoes on all the women in the kingdom. When we find the feet that fit these shoes, we'll have found our brides-to-be!"

Rupert looked at his brother with disbelief. "That is positively amazing," he said, "the most amazingly dumb idea I've ever heard. You could end up married to a toad! I have a much better idea." But Randolph wouldn't listen. He ran to his room to get his beauty sleep.

The next day he put his plan into action. He went to every house in the kingdom, trying to cram women's feet into the glass slipper.

Rupert, too, put his plan into action. First he looked up all the Ednas in the palace directory. Then he visited them and asked each one this question: "How many recipes do you know for tuna casserole?"

Randolph soon became discouraged. All the feet he saw were either too large, too wide, too long, or adorned with electric pink toenail polish.

Rupert, too, was discouraged. While some Ednas could name tuna casserole with pecan sauce, and others could name tuna casserole with sour cream and rice, no one could name more than seven kinds of tuna casserole.

Finally Randolph got to Cinderella's house. The cruel stepsisters were eager to try on the glass slipper, but, of course, it didn't fit either of them.

Suddenly Randolph noticed a woman in rags, sitting forlornly among the cinders in the corner. Something about her seemed familiar.

"Oh, Miss. Why don't you try this on?" he suggested. With trembling hands, Cinderella tried on the glass slipper. It fit perfectly!

Randolph swept her up in his arms and carried her away to the palace so that they could be married.

Meanwhile Rupert reached Cinder Edna's house. Her wicked stepsisters wanted to try on the loafer, but Rupert wouldn't let them because they weren't named Edna.

At that moment, Cinder Edna came in from mowing the lawn. Her heart almost stopped when she saw Rupert. He blinked nearsightedly at her.

Without his glasses Cinder Edna looked something like a large plate of mashed potatoes.

"Are you, let's see ... Ashes Edna?" he asked, peering closely at his list of names. "No, I already talked to her." He wasn't sure these Ednas with an extra name counted, but he had already tried the just plain Ednas.

"*Cinder.* Cinder Edna," she said.

"Oh. Well, can you name sixteen different kinds of tuna casserole?"

"Of course," she said, and she began to name them. She rattled off fifteen different kinds, including tuna casserole with pickled pigs feet, and then she stopped. What was that last one anyway?

"Only fifteen," said Rupert, turning to go.

"Well, maybe I can't name sixteen kinds of tuna casserole," said Edna. "But I *do* know a great joke about a kangaroo from Kalamazoo."

Rupert stopped in his tracks.

"My love!" he said. He gave her a kiss. "Will you marry me?"

Soon after that, Randolph and Ella (she dropped the cinder part) and Rupert and Edna (she did the same) were married in a grand double ceremony.

So the girl who had once been known as Cinderella ended up in a big palace. During the day she went to endless ceremonies and listened to dozens of speeches by His Highness the Grand Archduke of Lethargia and the Second Deputy Underassistant of Underwear. And at night she sat by the fire with nothing to look at but her husband's perfect profile while he talked endlessly of troops, parade formations, and uniform buttons.

And the girl who had been known as Cinder Edna ended up in a small cottage with solar heating. During the day she studied waste disposal engineering and cared for orphaned kittens. And at night she and her husband laughed and joked, tried new recipes together, and played duets on the accordion and concertina.

Guess who lived happily ever after.

AFTER YOU READ

Make a comparison chart

Make a chart to compare how Cinderella, Cinder Edna, and you react when you have an undesirable experience. Compare thoughts, feelings, and actions.

Rick Hansen:
No Walls Too Big to Climb

■ ■ ■ ■

Written by Mary Beth Leatherdale

READING TIP

Think about your experiences

Think of a time when you set a personal goal. What happened? As you read, record what Rick Hansen did to achieve his personal goal to tour the world and raise awareness of the barriers that disabled people face.

Rick Hansen dreamed of doing the impossible. He dreamed of wheeling around the world—a distance of 40 000 kilometres—in his wheelchair. And through blinding snowstorms, over tall mountain ranges, and against other countless obstacles, Vancouver-born Rick Hansen travelled across 34 countries and made his dream a reality.

Rick's idea of wheeling around the world grew slowly. At first, Rick was just interested in challenging himself physically. When he was 15 years old, he was hitching a ride in the back of a truck when it went out of control. The resulting injury to Rick's spinal cord left him paralyzed from the waist down, meaning he would never walk again.

LEARNING GOALS

You will

- read about a man who had a goal to travel around the world to raise money for spinal cord research

- compare your experiences with goal-setting with those of Rick Hansen

Rick had always enjoyed sports, so after the accident he started coaching and eventually began participating in wheelchair marathons. He won 19 wheelchair marathons in a row and became world champion three times. His success in marathoning made him realize that he might be physically and emotionally strong enough to take on the challenge of wheeling around the world—if he wanted to.

Rick had trained with and become friends with another disabled athlete named Terry Fox. Terry had lost his leg to cancer. In 1980, Terry set off to run across Canada; Terry's Marathon of Hope was intended to focus attention on cancer and raise funds for cancer research. Rick was inspired by Terry's courage and what he achieved. Rick realized that he too could raise awareness of the physical and mental barriers that disabled people face. And a world tour would give him the opportunity to raise money for research, rehabilitation, and wheelchair sport and recreation programs

for people with spinal cord injuries.

So Rick decided to make his dream a reality. Planning for his Man in Motion tour was a huge undertaking. What route would he take? Where would he sleep? What would he eat? What kind of safety, medical, and training gear would he need? Who would help him during the tour? How would he make sure he was safe on the road? And where would he get the money to start the tour?

Despite working to overcome these obstacles for over a year, Rick never considered giving up. As he told a sports writer: "We're committed to this thing! If it turns out that [crew members] Tim and Don and I have to leave in a Volkswagen Beetle with three sleeping bags and the wheelchair in the back, then that's the way it will be. I'm going to wheel that chair around the world and that's all there is to it."

Finally on March 21, 1985, Rick set off from Vancouver, British Columbia, to wheel around the world. But his problems were not over. From early in the tour, Rick faced difficult weather conditions—wheeling against strong winds and rain, day after day. Then Rick started to have pain in his hands. Rick thought the pain was caused by mechanical problems with his wheelchair so he had his crew try adjusting the seat of his

wheelchair by tiny amounts, dropping it one quarter of a centimetre or moving it forward by a half a centimetre. While these adjustments would help the pain in one spot it would put strain on the other hand or wrist, causing more problems. Rick knew if he didn't take care of the injuries and continued wheeling he might have to take a break from—or even cancel—the tour until his injuries were healed. But through careful management and help from his physiotherapist and girlfriend Amanda Reid, Rick was able to continue.

Rick's world tour was not a fun-filled adventure. While he visited famous cities such as London, Paris, and Moscow, the many scheduled appearances and the physical demands of wheeling gave him very little time or energy to sightsee or get to know these places.

But his visit to China was a dream come true. The night before Rick began the world tour a friend asked him, "What do you want to get out of this tour?" Rick responded, "When I come back and it's all over, I want to be able to wake up in the morning, look at the bedroom wall, and see a picture of me in the wheelchair, sitting on the Great Wall of China."

"That's it?" his friend asked.

"That's it. I want to be able to lie there for a minute, and stare at it, and remember what it took to get there, and remind myself that there are no walls too big to climb." Rick did climb the Great Wall of China, an incredible achievement. It was extremely difficult because of the very steep angle of the Great Wall.

When Rick returned to Vancouver on May 22, 1987—more than two years after he set out on the Man in Motion tour—a crowd of 50 000 people greeted him. He had become a celebrity recognized around the globe and had raised more than $20 million for spinal cord research, rehabilitation, and recreation programs. By proving to himself that there are no walls too big to climb, he had also demonstrated this belief to countless others and inspired them.

AFTER YOU READ

Make connections

Review the information you recorded from the story. Make a chart to show connections between a time when you achieved a personal goal and Rick Hansen's process of achieving his goal.

Sportsmanship
And Other Etiquette Tips ...

From Kids' Wall Street News *magazine*
Illustrated by Tina Holdcroft

Winner or Loser
Spectator or Participant
Good Sportsmanship Requires ...
Patience
Tolerance
Cooperation
Courtesy

Do ...
- Be a team player
- Keep cool
- Play for the sake of playing, not just to win
- Keep your temper under control
- Appreciate the talents of others
- Congratulate the winners

Right!

Don't ...
- Shout insults
- Complain
- Gloat or brag
- Make excuses for losing
- Sulk
- Argue with the officials
- Make fun of the losing team

Personal Best

Note use of punctuation and capitalization

Poets often use punctuation and capitalization in unusual ways to help you read and understand poems. Scan the following poems and note how the poets have used punctuation and capitalization as an important part of their poems.

DIVING BOARD

Written and illustrated by Shel Silverstein

You've been up on that diving board
Making sure that it's nice and straight.
You've made sure that it's not too slick.
You've made sure it can stand the weight.
You've made sure that the spring is tight.
You've made sure that the cloth won't slip.
You've made sure that it bounces right,
And that your toes can get a grip—
And you've been up there since half past five
Doin' everything ... but DIVE.

The Spearthrower

Written by Lillian Morrison
Illustrated by Scott Medlock

She walks alone
to the edge of the park
and throws into
the bullying dark
her javelin
of light,
her singing sign
her signed song
that the runner may run
far and long

her quick laps
on the curving track
that the sprinter surge
and the hurdler leap
that the vaulter soar,
clear the highest bar,
and the discus fly
as the great crowds cry
to their heroines
Come on!

Lonnie Boo

Written by Isaac L. Maefield
Illustrated by Leon Zernitsky

    I came to play
I twirl and pearl/dribble the ball
behind my back/between my legs.
    Why, I jump so high
sometimes I need a parachute to land safely.
They used to call me UFO
because the Air Force radar
thought I was from outer space.
    I can run so fast that one time,
during a game, I ran to the store,
bought a juice/drank it
and got back before anyone knew I was gone
... And I had the ball.
    I helicoptered around
and dunked so hard, I tore the basket down.
    My name is Lonnie Boo
and I CAN DO THE DO.

When I Grow Up

Written by LeRoy Gorman

I want to be a—
     ph?losopher
     p!tcher
     space*man
     sk%nd%ver
     co"me"dian
but not a—
     solDIEr
     ¢ounterf$tter
     cyclOps
     (alien)
     cclloonnee
& especially not a—
     Xeacher

AFTER YOU READ

Think like an author

Make a list of the punctuation used in the poems. Why do you think the poets used punctuation in this way? What kind of response do you think the poets were trying to get from their readers?

The Killick

Written and illustrated by Geoff Butler
Excerpted from The Killick: A Newfoundland Story

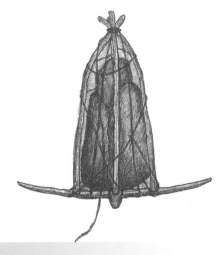

READING TIP

Think about what you already know

Think about some heroes that you know from your personal experiences, from reading, or from television. Make a list of characteristics that you think these heroes have in common. As you read, compare Skipper Fred to your list of criteria.

A killick is a homemade anchor put together by placing rocks inside a cage of wood. It stands for many things in this story of courage from Newfoundland.

Spring has come and George sails with his grandfather to an abandoned fishing outport so the old man can visit his wife's grave. Newfoundlanders served and died in awesome numbers in the two World Wars and the grandfather brings along the medals his wife took such pride in.

LEARNING GOALS

You will

- read about how a boy and his grandfather try to survive when they are stranded on an ice pan

- find evidence to support your opinion

On the way back to the boat, they wave to Isaac as they pass his house.

Skipper Fred still wants to talk about his wife. "You know, we were comrades-in-arms. And we were comrades in life, too, which is even more important. Did I ever tell you, when I came to in the field hospital after they lopped off my leg, she was the first person I saw? She was holding my hand and smiling. 'I'm from Newfoundland, too,' her first words were. I'd never seen her before, thought maybe I'd gone to heaven, she was so beautiful. Did I ever tell you that, George?"

George had heard it before. His grandfather was fond of telling it, as if he relived the moment each time. Instead of answering, George says: "I was reading dates on the gravestones, Grandpa. People died young then, didn't they?"

"Yes," Skipper Fred says. "For all the good times back then, it was a hard life and little doctoring. We had to travel in summer by boat or in winter by horse and sleigh on the ice to get to a doctor. It was better after the war when your grandma started nursing up and down the coast. The cottage hospitals were around and health care was in better shape."

They reach the stage. George helps his grandfather into the boat. "We'll be back in time for a game of checkers before supper, George. Now, open her up, boy."

George starts the motor and points the bow homeward. As the boat picks up speed, he notices pans of ice floating about.

It is smooth going for a while, but, farther out, the seas get rougher and they get into their rain gear to protect themselves from the spray off the bow and the tops of waves that leap over the gunwales.

They are well in the bay when the trouble starts. The engine sputters and, after a few asthmatic gasps, dies out. The boat drifts as George tries to restart the motor.

The wind, shifting about, starts to bring in a few snowflakes. George keeps struggling desperately with the motor. He realizes they are in for some bad weather. He considers rowing, but Skipper Fred motions toward the sail and starts to crawl forward. He shouts out: "We'll run with the wind, George, and put ashore further down. Keep a firm hand on the tiller. With any luck, we'll stay ahead of the ice."

Skipper Fred loosens the sail as George tries to keep the rudder steady. But the wind quickly brings in more ice

that slams against the dory. The snow is now so heavy, George can hardly see his grandfather trying to work the sail.

The dory is tossed violently against jagged slabs of ice. Suddenly, there is an ominous crunch as the hull is pierced. Then, just as quickly, a swirling squall catches the sail and lifts them. More ice moves in and becomes wedged under the other side of the dory.

George scrambles onto the ice and helps his grandfather get out. Together they pry up the dory with the oars, inch by inch, using the killick as the fulcrum. They

stabilize the boat against the wind and get in under it, huddling together.

The wind howls and the snow swirls around them. But at last, with their heads close together, they can hear each other speak.

"Not to worry, George," Skipper Fred says, his arms around his grandson. "We seem to be on a sizeable ice floe. When we don't show up for supper, there'll be a search party on its way. I don't think we'll be going anywhere like this. At least not down." He hugs George tighter. "Are you warm enough?"

"How will a search party ever find us?" George asks. "The weather and the seas will be too bad for them to even leave home."

"Be that as it may, George, they'll find us soon enough. We're safe here on the ice, so let's just concentrate on staying warm." He takes some hard-tack from his pocket, holds it out to George, and grins: "Care for some supper?"

George realizes his grandfather is trying to sound encouraging, but the wind has changed direction and he is scared. How far out to sea, how far away from land is the ice floe being pushed? Will the ice hold under them? He tries to remember being in this kind of trouble before, but he can't.

They settle in as best they can, huddling together in their windbreak. Time goes by slowly. The snow becomes so thick at times they can barely see out. Darkness sets in. Skipper Fred dozes off, but George is too scared to sleep.

He remembers an old fisherman describing how he once sat in a lifeboat, wondering if he'd be rescued. "When there's nothing you can do except wait and hope, think of something you're proud you did. We Newfoundlanders have no trouble with that, do we?" But George had never known war or danger to be brave in. What could he be proud of, he wonders. Maybe of laying that wreath after a classmate had made fun of him when he said he was going to. The words still hurt:

> Georgie, porgie, pudding and pie
> Sat on a poppy and cried and cried.
> In Flanders fields, he dropped the torch
> And now his underwear is scorched.
> Pudgy Georgie runs away
> When the real boys come out to play.

When George told his mother about it, she had said that sticks and stones break bones, but names never hurt. But his grandfather had interrupted. "Names do hurt," he had said. "My father was hurt when he was called a barbarian. And in war, it's easier to kill people by calling them names. Makes them seem not like real people."

George was proud he decided to go ahead and lay that wreath, no matter how much he was ridiculed. Maybe a wreath can commemorate the innocent victims of war on both sides.

The next day, the weather remains fierce. There'll be no one out looking for them in this. They sit in their shelter, waiting and listening for the wind to drop. How far out to sea have they been swept by now?

Suddenly, Skipper Fred holds up his hand: "I thought I heard seals barking out on the ice." He listens again: "It can't be. It's too late in the spring. They'll have gone north."

Later, the snow lets up a little but the wind is still strong. Now and then there is the cracking sound of ice splitting up. George can feel the small pan moving under them, like a raft carrying them further out to sea.

"Hand me the oar there, George," Skipper Fred says. He pulls himself up and goes outside the shelter, using the oar to balance himself. George watches him move about the ice, poking it every so often to see how strong it is.

As another night approaches, the sound of water lapping around the edges of the ice becomes clearer. How much longer can the pan support the weight of the two of them? George asks if they should nudge the boat off if the

pan gets smaller, but his grandfather shakes his head. They need it for shelter from the wind.

His grandfather wants to talk: "I've been thinking, George. When it's my time to go, I want you to use a killick for my tombstone. Put it beside my wife's stone. It's a proper marking for an old fisherman. Besides, a killick's made of sticks and stones. That wreath you laid for all the innocent victims of war, I'd like the killick to commemorate them, too, all those nameless people that were called names."

His grandfather fumbles about in his pocket for his medals. George watches as the old man rubs his cold hands

together before managing awkwardly to pin the medals to his rain jacket.

They settle in for another night. George does not mention how hungry he is as he tries to sleep.

Suddenly and unexpectedly, the ice pan surges forward, jarring George awake. His grandfather is no longer beside him.

"Grandpa, Grandpa," he shouts. He moves out of the boat shelter, looks around and sees that he is alone.

As the weather gradually lets up during the morning, George sees how small the ice pan has gotten and realizes what his grandfather had done for him.

Miserably, he sits watching pans of ice floating about, rocking back and forth with the waves on the cold, grey water, and remembering the words his grandfather had used the day before, he realizes it was his grandfather's way of saying goodbye.

"The crests and troughs of the sea," he had said, "are like a rocking cradle, George, and that's what nourished the Newfoundland culture. Over the centuries, it rocked and rocked, moulding the Newfoundland character, which knows as well as any that the sea which gives so much is also merciless in what it takes. The sea tests the courage of a man."

Toward afternoon, George hears the put-put-put of a motor in the distance. He stands up and waves his arms frantically.

Before long, he is drinking hot cocoa in the cabin of a rescue boat and is heading back home, with the killick of his grandfather's dory at his feet.

AFTER YOU READ

Give evidence

Was Skipper Fred a hero? Write a paragraph to support your opinion. Give evidence from the story and from your list of criteria about what makes a hero. Do you think George was a hero?

Illustrations taken from *The Killick* © 1995 Geoff Butler. Published by Tundra Books.

The People Who Hugged the Trees

Adapted by Deborah Lee Rose
Illustrated by Birgitta Säflund

READING TIP

Make predictions

Use the title and the illustrations to predict what the story will be about. Use the information from the story to confirm or revise your predictions.

In long-ago India, when warrior princes ruled the land, there lived a girl who loved the trees. Her name was Amrita.

Amrita lived in a poor village of mud houses, on the edge of the great desert. Just outside the village grew a forest.

LEARNING GOALS

You will

- learn about a girl who stood up to others to achieve her goal

- make predictions by previewing the title and the illustrations

Every day Amrita ran to the forest, her long braid dancing behind her. When she found her favourite tree, she threw her arms around it. "Tree," she cried, "you are so tall and your leaves are so green! How could we live without you?" For Amrita knew that the trees shaded her from the hot desert sun. The trees guarded her from the howling desert sandstorms. And where the trees grew, there was precious water to drink. Before she left the forest, Amrita kissed her special tree. Then she whispered, "Tree, if *you* are ever in trouble, I will protect you."

The tree whispered back with a rustle of its leaves.

One day just before the monsoon rains, a giant sandstorm whirled in from the desert. In minutes the sky turned dark as night. Lightning cracked the sky and wind whipped the trees as Amrita dashed for her house. From inside, she could hear the sand battering against the shutters. After the storm ended, there was sand everywhere—in Amrita's clothes, in her hair, and even in her food.

But she was safe and so was her village, because the trees had stood guard against the worst of the storm.

As Amrita grew, so did her love for the trees. Soon she had her own children, and she took them to the forest with her.

"These are your brothers and sisters," she told them. "They shade us from the hot desert sun. They guard us from the terrible desert sandstorms. They show us where to find water to drink," she explained. Then Amrita taught her children to hug the trees as she did.

Each day when she left the forest, Amrita fetched water from the village well. She carried the water in a large clay pot balanced on top of her head.

One morning by the well, Amrita spotted a troop of men armed with heavy axes. They were headed toward the forest. "Cut down every tree you can find," she heard the chief axeman say. "The Maharajah needs plenty of wood to build his new fortress."

The Maharajah was a powerful prince who ruled over many villages. His word was law. Amrita was afraid. "The tree-cutters will destroy our forest," she thought. "Then we will have no shade from the sun or protection from the sandstorms. We will have no way to find water in the desert!"

Amrita ran to the forest and hid. From her hiding place, she could hear the *whack* of the axes cutting into her beloved trees.

Suddenly Amrita saw the chief axeman swing his blade toward her special tree.

"Do not cut down these trees!" she cried and jumped in front of her tree. "Stand back!" thundered the axeman. "Please, leave my tree," Amrita begged. "Chop me instead." She hugged the tree with all her strength. The axeman shoved her away and swung his blade.

He could see only the tree he had been ordered to cut. Again and again the axeman chopped until Amrita's tree crashed to the ground. Amrita knelt down, her eyes filled with tears. Her arms tenderly grasped the tree's dying branches.

When news of Amrita's tree reached the village, men, women, and children came running to the forest. One after another they jumped in front of the trees and hugged them. Wherever the tree-cutters tried to chop, the villagers stood in their way.

"The Maharajah will hear of this!" threatened the chief axeman.

But the people would not give in.

The Maharajah was furious when the axemen returned
emptyhanded. "Where is the wood I sent you to chop?" he
stormed. "Your Highness, we tried to cut down the trees for

your fortress," answered the chief axeman. "But wherever we went, the villagers hugged the trees to stop us."

The Maharajah sliced the air with his battle sword. "These tree-huggers will pay for disobeying me!" He mounted his fastest horse and rode out for the forest. Behind him came many soldiers, riding long-legged camels and elephants with jewelled tusks.

The Maharajah found the people gathered by the village well.

"Who has dared to defy my order?" he demanded. Amrita hesitated a moment, then she stepped forward.

"Oh Great Prince, we could not let the axemen destroy our forest," she said. "These trees shade us from the baking desert sun. They protect us from the sandstorms that would kill our crops and bury our village. They show us where to find precious water to drink."

"Without these trees I cannot build a strong fortress!" the Maharajah insisted.

"Without these trees we cannot survive," Amrita replied.

The Maharajah glared at her.

"Cut them down!" he shouted.

The villagers raced to the forest as the soldiers flashed their swords. Step by step the soldiers drew closer, as the sand swirled around their feet and the leaves shivered on the trees. Just when the soldiers reached the trees the wind roared in from the desert, driving the sand so hard they could barely see.

The soldiers ran from the storm, shielding themselves behind the trees. Amrita clutched her special tree and the villagers hid their faces as thunder shook the forest. The storm was worse than any the people had ever known. Finally, when the wind was silent, they came slowly out of the forest.

Amrita brushed the sand from her clothes and looked around. Broken tree limbs were scattered everywhere. Grain from the crops in the field littered the ground.

Around the village well drifts of sand were piled high, and Amrita saw that only the trees had stopped the desert from destroying the well and the rest of the village.

Just beyond the well the Maharajah stood and stared at the forest. He thought for a long time, then he spoke to the villagers.

"You have shown great courage and wisdom to protect your trees. From this day on your trees will not be cut," the Maharajah declared.

"Your forest will always remain a green place in the desert."

The people rejoiced when they heard the Maharajah's words. They sang and danced long into the night and lit up the sky with fireworks.

In the forest, the children strung flowers and bright coloured paper through the branches of the trees. And where Amrita's tree had fallen, they marked a special place so they would never forget the tree's great sacrifice.

Many years have passed since that day, but some people say Amrita still comes to the forest to hug the trees.

"Trees," she whispers, "you are so tall and your leaves are so green! How could we live without you?"

For Amrita knows that the trees shade the people from the hot desert sun.

The trees guard the people from the howling desert sandstorms.

And where the trees grow there is water, and it is a good place for the people to live.

AFTER YOU READ

Record your predictions and findings

Use a chart like the one below to record your predictions and findings. Using the information from the story, record your responses in the three columns.

My Predictions	Evidence that Confirmed My Predictions	Evidence that Made Me Reject My Predictions

Going the Distance

In this unit, you have learned about the different ways people set goals and strive for their "personal best." You have read about the obstacles others faced while working to achieve their goals. Now it is your turn to set a personal goal for yourself. You will develop a plan to achieve your goal and write a poem to encourage and inspire yourself.

▶ Before You Begin

Your personal goal could be about a career or something you would like to do.

Think about what kind of personal goal you would like to set for the future. Ask yourself these questions:

- What plans will I have to make to achieve my goal?
- Do I need special training or education?
- Do I need to do some research to find out more information?
- What obstacles could I face?
- What one thing could I do right now to help me start toward my goal?

What to Include in Your Plan

- ▶ a clear statement of your goal
- ▶ an action plan
- ▶ possible challenges
- ▶ action required to meet challenges
- ▶ your thoughts about reaching your goal

Here are some examples of long-term goals set by other students your age.

My long-term goal is to be in the Olympics in figure skating. I practise 3-4 days a week. It's not always easy waking up at 6 am. For the next few years I am going to reach for the sky to reach this goal!

Alexis Eapen

My long-term goal is to be an architect.

I think you need to be accurate, precise, and creative. I want to be an architect because it's fun and challenging. My best work was drawing my house.

Andrew Schurman

▶ Make a Plan

1 **Choose a way to set out your plan to achieve your goal.**

- Choose a visual you can look at every day that will remind you of your goal.
- Think of ways your plan can visually inspire you.

Seul Kee chose to represent her goal in a poster.

Remember to put your plan in a place where you can see it every day.

2 **Choose a goal.**

- Write a statement that clearly explains your goal.

3 **Write an action plan.**

- Think of all the steps you will have to take in order to achieve your goal.
- Make a list of the actions you can take now, next month, next year, and five years from now.

Here is an example of Alexis's action plan.

Remember, action plans are written in the order the actions will take place. Each step in the plan should have a target date for when it will be accomplished.

> My Action Plan for Becoming an Olympic Figure Skater
>
> Actions I can take now: Keeping my back straight for all spins and jumps
>
> Actions I can take next month: Knowing I can do my best at the Provincial Competition. I'm going to focus on landing my jumps accurately.

▶ Your First Draft

Refer to your action plan and draft a personal poem that can encourage you to attain your goal. Achieving a goal can be difficult, so the encouragement your writing can bring is important.

1 **Identify the obstacles.**
- Predict what obstacles and challenges you might meet as you work to achieve your goal.
- Make a list of these challenges.

> My long term goal: Architect
>
> My challenges:
> ·giving the people what they want or as close as possible
> ·designing sky scraper
> ·getting creative blueprints
> ·designing space stations
> ·building my own home

Here are some of the obstacles Andrew predicted he would face.

2 **Plan to overcome obstacles.**
- Think carefully about each obstacle or challenge you have identified.
- Beside each obstacle, record a possible action or solution to the problem.

3 **Record your thoughts and feelings.**
- Think about how you will feel when you reach your goal. Record the words that best describe how you will feel.
- Include these feelings in your poem.

4 **Write your poem.**

Here is part of a poem Laura wrote about her personal goal.

> My Writing Journey
> Author: Laura Chow
>
> When I write a book
> I think of my feelings and opinions
> I put them into ideas
> I think of the kind of books I like
> And try to capture my audience's attention
> I practise writing most of the time.

Where to Post Your Goal Poem

- computer screen-saver
- bedroom door
- fridge
- locker
- bulletin board

▶ Put It All Together

Add a visual to the poem you wrote. It might be an illustration from your imagination about achieving your goal. It might be a decorative border to highlight your goal poem.

Be expressive in the way you write and illustrate your poem.

bold △ *italics*
thin wide ✳

Revise and Edit

Go back and review what you have included in your plan and in your poem.

- Look carefully at your plan. Are there ways to improve what you have done?
- Get feedback from two friends. Ask them to talk about two things they like about your work and one thing you might change to make it more effective.
- Is your poem meaningful and inspiring?
- Proofread for grammar, spelling, and punctuation.
- Check for neatness.

Think about Your Learning

Add your own ideas to what makes a good visual representation of your learning.

- Did you choose a long-term goal?
- Did you make your plan to achieve your goal clear?
- Did your plan include a date for meeting your goal?
- Did you write your poem in a way that will focus you on your goal?
- Does your poem's design catch your attention?
- Did you use powerful and inspiring words?

Unit 2: *Searching for Evidence*

Whenever you want to find out information you have many sources to go and search. You can ask someone, or read a book, or go to a library, or watch a video, or use the Internet. But have you ever wondered where all of this information comes from—or how people discovered this information? In this unit, you will find out how scientists, historians, and doctors search for information. You will discover some of the methods and tools that are used to provide you with answers about yourself, your world, other worlds, and your past. You will

- read a variety of information materials, such as articles, a journal, poems, and a story
- learn to gather information from graphics such as diagrams and photographs
- take notes while reading information selections
- use a variety of charts and webs to organize information
- pick out the main idea and details in information selections
- learn to use different reading strategies to help you read information materials
- search for evidence as you write your own research report

Space Songs

Written by Myra Cohn Livingston
Illustrated by Jean-Pierre Normand

Satellites

Monitors of steel,
these space detectives seek
clues to the beginning of our galaxy.
Informers of the energy of stars, of gamma rays;
weighted with sensors,
They listen, watch, and speak
of radiation, solar flares,
atmospheric density,
Stalking magnetic fields,
they serve out their days.

80

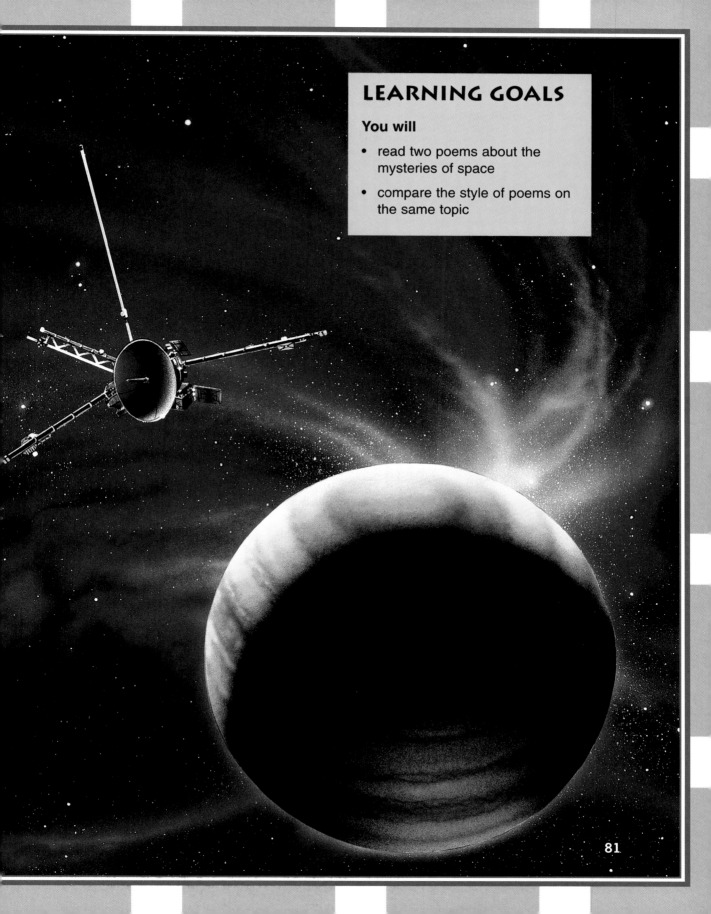

LEARNING GOALS

You will

- read two poems about the mysteries of space

- compare the style of poems on the same topic

81

Secrets

Space keeps its secrets
                    hidden.

It does not tell.

          Are black holes time machines?
          Where do lost comets go?

          Is Pluto moon or planet?

How many, how vast
          unknown galaxies beyond us?

          Do other creatures
          dwell   on distant spheres?

                              Will we ever know?

Space is silent.
It seldom answers.

          But we ask.

AFTER YOU READ

Make comparisons

Make a chart like the one below to compare the techniques used by the poet in each of the two poems. Which poem spoke most clearly to you about the mysteries of space?

	Words	Shape	Sound
Satellites			
Secrets			

Mars Pathfinder

Written by Ray Jayawardhana
From Muse *magazine*
Illustrated by Bart Vallecoccia

READING TIP

Find the main ideas

When reading for information, it is a good idea to jot down notes about the main ideas. Each paragraph has one main idea that will give you information about the topic. As you read each paragraph, stop and write down a few words—in point form—to remind you of the main idea.

In July 1997, Mars had a special visitor from Earth. It was a spacecraft called *Mars Pathfinder* and it was launched by NASA on December 4, 1996. *Pathfinder* took seven months to reach Mars and landed on July 4, 1997.

Pathfinder was the first spacecraft to arrive at Mars since the twin *Vikings* landed there 21 years earlier. Its destination was a rocky plain on Mars called *Ares Vallis*. Scientists believe that water may have flowed there over a billion years ago.

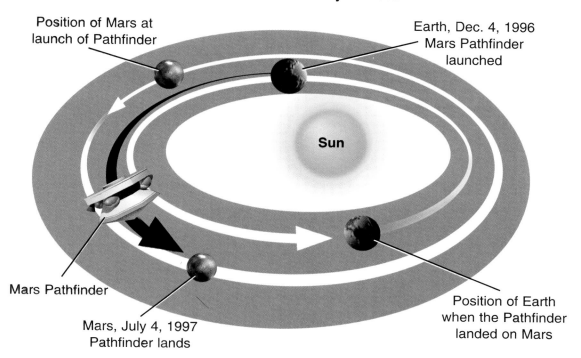

The Pathfinder's Journey to Mars

Position of Mars at launch of Pathfinder

Earth, Dec. 4, 1996
Mars Pathfinder launched

Sun

Mars Pathfinder

Mars, July 4, 1997
Pathfinder lands

Position of Earth when the Pathfinder landed on Mars

Before NASA scientists launched the Pathfinder they had to plan how far and how fast it would have to travel in order to reach Mars as the planet moved along its orbit.

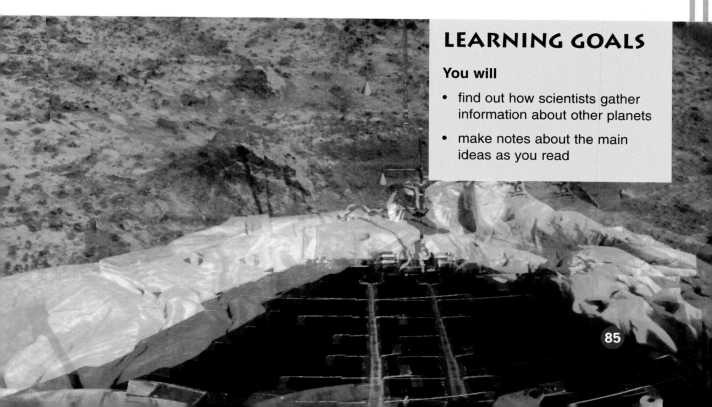

LEARNING GOALS

You will

- find out how scientists gather information about other planets

- make notes about the main ideas as you read

There has never been a landing quite like *Pathfinder*'s. It headed straight to the planet's surface, instead of circling it first, as the *Vikings* and the *Apollo* missions to the Moon did. Then a parachute opened and slowed *Pathfinder* down as it plunged through the Martian atmosphere. About 20 m before it hit the surface, the parachute dropped away and large air bags inflated to cushion the impact. The spacecraft bounced three times until it came to rest. *Pathfinder*'s computers then deflated the bags. Two ramps popped out, and a remote-controlled six-wheeled buggy, no bigger than a microwave oven, rolled down to take a look around. This rover, called *Sojourner*, inspected Martian rocks and sent live pictures of the planet's surface to Earth.

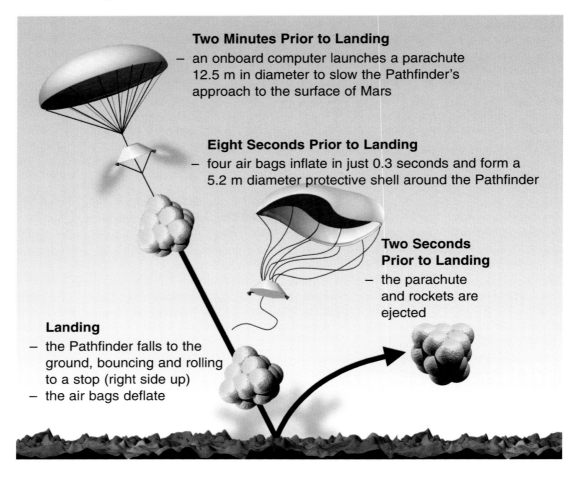

Two Minutes Prior to Landing
– an onboard computer launches a parachute 12.5 m in diameter to slow the Pathfinder's approach to the surface of Mars

Eight Seconds Prior to Landing
– four air bags inflate in just 0.3 seconds and form a 5.2 m diameter protective shell around the Pathfinder

Two Seconds Prior to Landing
– the parachute and rockets are ejected

Landing
– the Pathfinder falls to the ground, bouncing and rolling to a stop (right side up)
– the air bags deflate

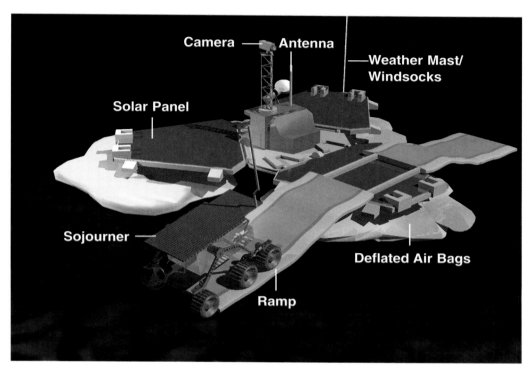

The Mars Pathfinder lander.

To make sure they could guide *Sojourner* around Mars's rocky surface, NASA scientists in California had been practising with a remote-controlled rover. After all, a wrong turn into a boulder could wreck it. The scientists practised in a sandbox (complete with lots of rocks) about the size of a living room. But guiding *Sojourner* on Mars wasn't quite as easy as moving a remote-controlled rover on Earth. Instructions to *Sojourner*—travelling at the speed of light, about 300 000 km/s—took over 10 minutes to get from Earth to Mars. That meant that when scientists watched what *Sojourner*'s cameras saw on a video screen here on Earth, they were actually watching what the rover saw 10 minutes ago! So, if they saw the rover heading toward a rock, it would take another 10 minutes before they could signal it to change its path or stop.

Scientists tested the rover on Earth before sending it to Mars.

So, more important than studying rocks or soil, the *Pathfinder* mission was really a test of a big idea—could engineers build a machine that could make some decisions on its own? *Sojourner* had been equipped with a special laser navigation system that tells it when to avoid deep holes and big rocks.

Sojourner transmitted data and images to Earth until October 7, although NASA engineers expected that it might only have enough power to transmit for a week. While it was there, NASA scientists transmitted its panoramic views of Mars over the World Wide Web, which gave many of us a chance to share in the excitement. This included daily Martian weather reports, too.

Pathfinder was only the first of many spacecraft that NASA hopes to send to Mars in the next decade. Another probe, *Global Surveyor*, was launched in November 1996 and began orbiting Mars in September 1997. *Global Surveyor* will make detailed maps of Mars so that scientists can choose good

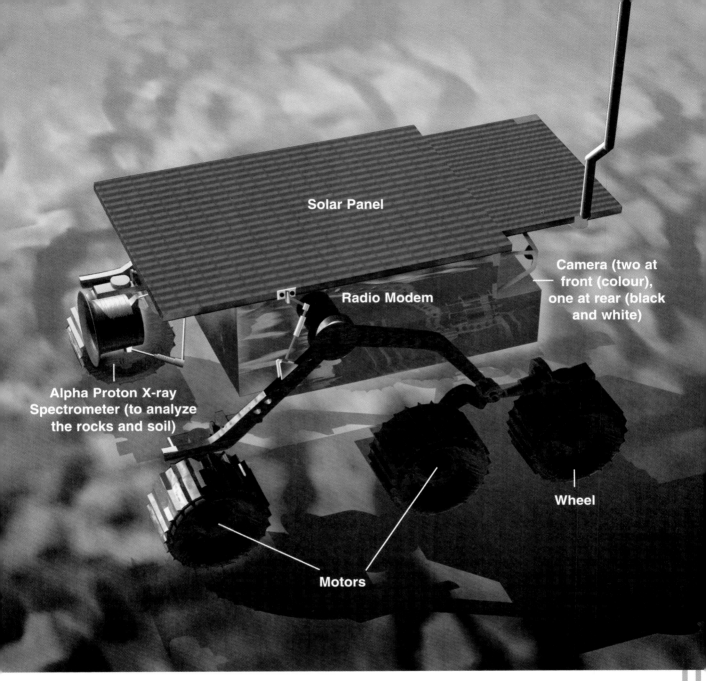

Solar Panel

Camera (two at front (colour), one at rear (black and white)

Radio Modem

Alpha Proton X-ray Spectrometer (to analyze the rocks and soil)

Wheel

Motors

A close-up look at the Pathfinder rover, the Sojourner.

landing sites for future missions. Eventually, NASA plans to send a spacecraft that will bring back samples of Martian soil. That could help them find out for sure whether any kind of life ever existed on Mars.

Above: One of the first pictures taken by a camera on the Pathfinder when it landed on Mars on July 4, 1997. **Below:** (left) The Sojourner on the surface of Mars. (right) A close-up view of a boulder on Mars.

The *Pathfinder* mission cost $US 280 million, about the same as making a big Hollywood movie. (OK, maybe *two* big Hollywood movies.) But the real-life mission proved to be more exciting than any made-up blockbuster. So with Mars on the web, sit back, relax, and enjoy the show!

AND NOW FOR THE Weather....

The climate on Mars, a planet long favoured by both scientists and science-fiction writers as a home for life, probably started out rather warm, but now it's in a deep freeze. Liquid water may have flowed on Mars long ago, but now its surface is dry and barren. The two *Viking* spacecraft which landed on Mars in 1976 didn't find any sign of life on its surface. If there were primitive life on Mars, it would only survive where the water is—underground and in the polar caps. In 1996, scientists discovered what may be fossils of ancient bacteria in a meteorite that is believed to have come from Mars. All the evidence isn't in yet, but it's quite possible that life existed on Mars in the remote past.

AFTER YOU READ

Summarize content

Make a web or chart that shows the topic—the Mars Pathfinder—and all of the main ideas you wrote down as you read. Each paragraph gives details to tell the reader more information about the main idea. Reread the selection and add important details to your web or chart.

The Case of the On-line Spaceman

Written by Seymour Simon
Excerpted from the novel The On-line Spaceman and Other Cases
Illustrated by Kim LaFave

READING TIP

Think about what you already know

Think about the detectives that you know—personally, through reading, or by watching television and movies. Make a list of the characteristics of a good detective. As you read, use your criteria to note whether or not Einstein is a good detective.

"It certainly doesn't feel like early autumn!" Einstein Anderson muttered to himself as he hurried down the dark road that led to Stanley's house. Einstein shivered as a cold September wind pushed against him. The shadowy tree branches whipped back and forth against one another, making strange crying sounds. The moon struggled to shine through the dark clouds overhead. Autumn had begun only a few days ago, but there was a chill in the air and a hint of snow in the clouds.

LEARNING GOALS

You will

- read about a boy who uses clues to solve a scientific mystery
- find out what techniques the author uses to develop his characters

93

If he walked fast, Einstein could get to Stanley's house in ten minutes. But most times it took him at least an hour, because he usually stopped to look at leaves, ants, spiders, birds, rotting logs, stars, and anything else that caught his eye. But tonight Einstein was in a hurry. Stanley had mentioned something about a strange thing that had happened and had asked Einstein to come over as quickly as he could.

Einstein Anderson was in sixth grade. He was thin, a bit taller than average height, and had dark hair. The eyeglasses he wore always seemed a bit too big for his face, and he was forever pushing them back when they slid down his nose. His brown eyes often had a faraway look, as if he were thinking about some interesting science experiment. But Einstein was not always serious. In fact, he loved a good joke—and even a bad one—and liked to make puns ... the worse, the better.

Einstein's real name was Adam. But few people called him that anymore. Adam had been interested in science and nature since he had learned how to talk. By the time he went to school, he could solve science mysteries that stumped even his teachers.

At the age of six, he had shared his knowledge about science with Ms. Moore, his kindergarten teacher. She was so impressed that she had given him the nickname of Einstein, after Albert Einstein, the most famous scientist of the twentieth century. Eventually, all his friends—and sometimes even his parents—called him Einstein.

By the time Einstein arrived at Stanley's house, he was breathing hard. He pressed the doorbell, and a strange voice boomed from behind the door. "Friend or foe?"

"It's me." Einstein's voice quavered a bit. That doesn't sound like Stanley. What in the world is going on? he thought.

"Friend or foe? Friend or foe? Friend or ggggrrrr...." The voice growled to a stop, and the door was flung open. A dark figure appeared at the entrance. Einstein had a small moment of panic before he recognized his friend.

"That dumb recording I made should stop after one announcement," Stanley complained. "I can't figure out why it keeps repeating itself." Stanley motioned Einstein to come in. "Why do you look so strange? And how come it took you so long to get here?" he asked impatiently.

"The journey, not the arrival, matters," Einstein smiled. "If you want to see time fly, throw your clock out the window."

Stanley groaned. He brushed his long black hair away from his face. "Stop telling me those corny jokes," he said. "This is serious. I think I have made an incredible discovery. I think I am in contact with an ET, an extraterrestrial. An encounter of the third kind. A lonely visitor from outer space. I'm usually very skeptical about space monsters, but this time I know it's true. Come on up to my laboratory, and I'll show you."

"You know why monster families stay together for so long? Because they can't stand to kiss each other goodbye," Einstein joked as he followed his friend upstairs. Stanley groaned again.

Stanley Roberts was a junior at Sparta Senior High School. Despite their age difference, Einstein and Stanley were good friends. Stanley was very interested in science and often invited Einstein to come over to his house to see his inventions and experiments.

Stanley pushed open the door to his "laboratory." It was really an attic room that his mom and dad had permitted him to use for his experiments. The room was a complete mess, as usual. Several computers hummed, their displays flickering in changing colours. Bunsen burners, glass test tubes, half-finished experiments, and strange-looking contraptions were everywhere. It looked like a junk shop, but Stanley insisted that it was all scientific apparatus.

"This is something really big-time," said Stanley. "An alien race will be able to tell me all kinds of things that no one on Earth knows. I'll become famous. And I'll build a great big laboratory, where I can do all kinds of neat experiments." He paused. "Einstein, my friend," Stanley continued, "I want you to help me contact this space visitor and share in my glory."

"Help you? How?" Einstein asked cautiously. He had the feeling that Stanley was setting him up to do something silly. He adjusted his glasses, and they promptly slid down again to the end of his nose. He pushed them back with one finger and said, "Are you sure this alien is real? The last time you asked me to help you with something like this, it turned out to be a phony baby Loch Ness monster."

"Forget about that," Stanley said impatiently. "This is something completely different. I have absolute proof. I got it from a new web site I found on the Internet."

"New web sites? Isn't that what you call two spiders who just got married? Newly webs?" Einstein asked with an innocent smile. He knew that a web site was a location on the worldwide telephone network called the Internet. Web sites usually displayed text and graphics and sometimes even sound and motion pictures. Einstein had used computer code to construct his own web site, on which he posted all kinds of interesting experiments and new discoveries in science.

"Your web site is not the only science on the Internet," Stanley said, ignoring Einstein's joke. "About a week ago, I was surfing the Internet, looking for new science experiments to do, when I came upon this strange web site. Here, let me show you."

Stanley sat down in front of one of his computers. His fingers flew across the keyboard as he connected to the Internet through the modem. The screen lit up with flashing red words spread against a background of twinkling stars. The words read: *Help! I am from a moon circling a planet that Earth astronomers call 70 Virginis B. My spaceship has crash-landed on your planet. Please contact me. I need your assistance to return to my home planet.*

"That's very interesting," said Einstein. "I read about the discovery of some new planets beyond the solar system. The first planetary system beyond our own was discovered in the early 1990s. Since then, a number of other planets have been discovered, including one called 70 Virginis B."

"What do we know about that planet?" asked Stanley. "Is it possible that life could come from there?"

"It's possible," replied Einstein cautiously. "The star, 70 Virginis, is very much like our sun. The planet discovered circling it is about eight times the mass of Jupiter.

Temperatures on the planet, or on any moons it might have, could possibly support life. In fact, some astronomers call the planet Goldilocks, because the temperature is 'just right' for liquid water to exist. But just because the so-called alien says he comes from there doesn't mean that he does."

"Don't you think I know that?" Stanley said, brushing back his black hair, which kept falling across his face. "But I wrote to the e-mail address on the web site, asking for some proof, and got a reply along with a computer file containing a scan of a photograph. Here, let me show it to you."

Stanley typed something on the keyboard, and a photo of a strange blue being appeared on the computer screen. Behind the blue creature was a weird-looking building. The blue figure certainly looked peculiar. Einstein bent down and peered at the screen more closely. The creature seemed to be holding up a placard that had some words written on it. "What do those words say?" Einstein asked.

"I couldn't make them out, either," said Stanley. "So I asked the alien to send me the original photo. It came in the mail today. Here it is. And here's the letter that came along with it. This creature—he calls himself a Klaatu—needs money to buy parts for his spaceship. He says that if I send him one hundred dollars, he will send me a scientific discovery that will make me famous. But the photo is blurry, and I still can't read the words on that sign that he's carrying. They seem to be in some kind of strange language."

Einstein picked up the photo and looked at it thoughtfully. "You know, Stanley, this photo might be a fake. This creature does look very strange, but for all we know, it could be a person in a pair of blue pyjamas and a mask. Nowadays, it's easy to fake a photo on a computer, and no one can tell whether it's real or not. In fact, many of the special effects in movies are put together on a computer. I'm not sure if there's any way you can prove it's real."

Einstein took out the magnifying lens that he carried with him and studied the photo. Then he looked at the same photo on the screen. He typed in several commands, and the photo became clearer. Then he played with the image, changing the colours and then reversing the photo, left to right. Suddenly his face broke into a huge smile, and he started to laugh. "I guess I can prove that this photo is a fake, after all," he said. He walked over to a mirror and held the photo in front of him. "Look at this, Stanley," he said.

"All I can see is your face in the mirror, grinning from ear to ear," said Stanley. "What am I supposed to be looking at?"

"Look at the writing on the sign," said Einstein. "This is just a hoax to get you to send money. I first saw it on the computer, but the mirror also lets you see what the sign says."

Can you solve the mystery:
How can a mirror help
Einstein read the words on
the "alien's" sign?

"I still don't see what you're talking about," said Stanley. "And what can a mirror show that I can't see just by looking at something?"

"A mirror does something very interesting," explained Einstein. "As you know, it reverses images from left to right. So if you write something on a piece of paper and look at it in a mirror, the writing looks backward."

"So what?" asked Stanley.

"Well, if you write something backward and then look at it in a mirror, it now appears the right way, and you can read it. So just read what is written on the sign this blue meanie is holding."

Stanley looked at the mirror image of the writing. Now he could make out what the words were: JOE'S DINER HAS MONSTROUSLY GOOD FOOD!

Stanley groaned and shook his head. "How could I have believed in that dumb picture? Just let me get my computer and write a letter to that blue spaceman!"

"Wait a minute." Einstein laughed. "If a spaceman is that blue, shouldn't you just try to cheer him up?"

AFTER YOU READ

Make a character sketch

Authors are like good detectives. They have to let their readers know what the characters in their stories are like in an interesting way. They do this by telling you about the character by what the character feels, says, and does, and by what others say about him or her. Make a list of the characteristics of Einstein and tell how you found out about these characteristics.

Looking Inside the Body

Written by Todd Mercer

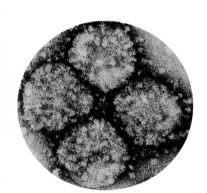

Close-up Views of the Human Body

Can you tell what these pictures are? They're all views of types of tiny germs that can live in people's bodies. The first picture is a tiny germ called a *virus.* Viruses cause infections like chicken pox. The second picture is a larger germ called a *bacterium.* Bacteria cause infections such as strep throat. The largest germ shown is a *parasite.* This one causes a sickness called Lyme disease.

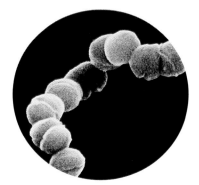

Not all germs are bad. In fact, you host many germs in your body.

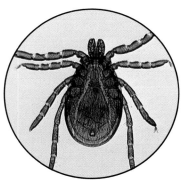

104

Did You Know?

▶ There are a million germs in your mouth!

▶ There are about 100 germs in your stomach. (That's because stomach acid kills many germs.)

LEARNING GOALS

You will

- find out how doctors learn about the inside of the human body
- gather information from pictures

Meet Dr. Anne Matlow

One person who's very interested in tiny hidden worlds within the human body is Dr. Anne Matlow. She's Director of Infection Control at the Hospital for Sick Children. Dr. Matlow is a medical doctor and a *microbiologist* ("micro" means small and "biologist" is a scientist who studies life). She is one of the physicians responsible for all the germ samples tested in the hospital's microbiology laboratory.

How does her work affect young patients? Here's just one example. If a child comes to the hospital's Emergency Department with a very sore throat, the examining doctor will probably ask for a *throat swab*, a sample of the germs at the back of the child's throat.

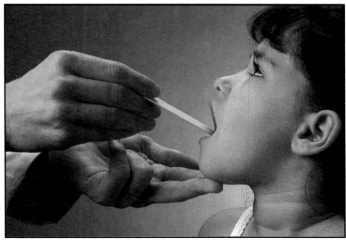

How Does a Medical Microbiologist Tell What's Wrong?

Germs are much smaller than what anyone could see with the human eye—even with the aid of a magnifying glass. When microbiologists or technologists at Dr. Matlow's laboratory receive a sample such as a throat swab, they prepare *plates* so they can look at the sample under a microscope.

To make a plate, they put the germ sample in a round dish and leave it to grow overnight.

The microbiologists can often identify the germ by closely observing how it grows.

Microscope plates, prepared for study under a microscope.

Many Kinds of Microscopes

There are four different types of microscopes in Dr. Matlow's laboratory. "Which ones we use," she explains, "depends on the type of germ we're trying to find."

"We have a light microscope to see an individual bacterium. The microscope can magnify the bacteria from 10 to 1000 times bigger than it really is."

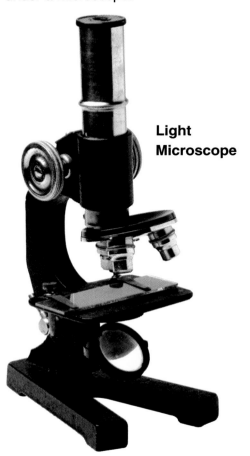

Light Microscope

"The stereomicroscope allows us to look at groups, or *colonies*, of bacteria. This lets us see more detail."

"We also have fluorescent microscopes in the lab. If we're looking for the germs that cause whooping cough, we add a fluorescent chemical to the germ sample. This chemical will only react with the whooping cough germ. If we see a glowing apple-green coloured reaction when we look at the plate through a fluorescent microscope, we know the patient has the whooping cough germ."

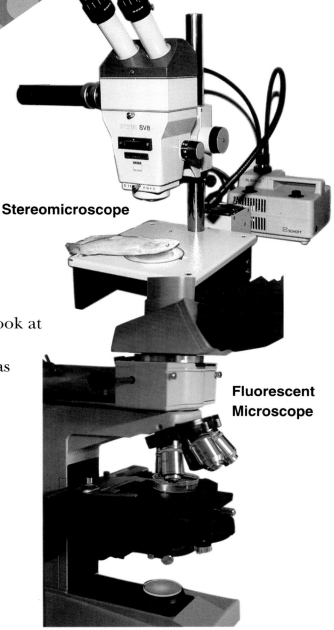

Stereomicroscope

Fluorescent Microscope

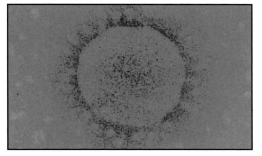

A virus, as seen through a fluorescent microscope.

A microorganism, as seen through an electron microscope.

"We might use an electron microscope to look at very tiny *viruses*, like the germ that causes chicken pox. Viruses are about 100 times smaller than bacteria. So we need more powerful microscopes to see them."

Controlling Germs

The major responsibility of medical microbiologists and technologists at the hospital laboratory is to diagnose infections. But they also have a second very important responsibility: they help physicians by determining the most effective medicines to use to treat infections or manage the infection-causing germs.

Usually we live in harmony with the germs in our body. (Remember those million germs living in your mouth.) But sometimes our germs grow out of control or harmful germs are introduced from other people, creatures, or the environment. And these often cause serious infections.

Maybe that's a good reason to listen when a parent or guardian says, "Wash your hands." You don't want to be responsible for passing germs you can't see to someone else.

Unfortunately infections do strike. And when they do, Dr. Matlow finds the most satisfying part of her work is "being able to diagnose and have an impact on the treatment of infections in children."

Maybe it's because of her experience as a medical doctor, but even when she's looking at the tiniest germ under a microscope, she's able to connect it to a person.

Other Doctors Who Have Close-up Views of the Human Body

Where are these views from? To find the answers, read the information below.

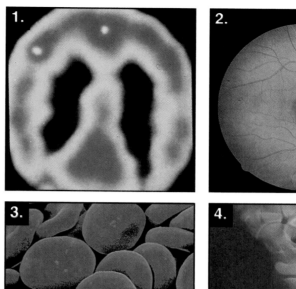

Eye Doctor

An eye doctor uses an ophthalmoscope to look in your eyes. He or she uses this tool to look at the size of your eye pupils and the backs of your eyes. If something is not normal, it may indicate a medical problem.

The eye doctor's close-up view is picture number two—a view of an eye pupil.

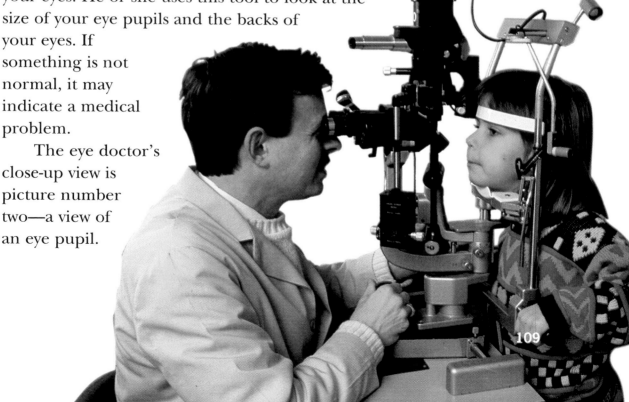

Radiologist

A radiologist is a doctor who interprets X-rays and other pictures taken of the inside of our bodies. For example, a radiologist would determine if you have a broken bone by "reading" your X-ray.

To make an X-ray of a broken leg, a special tube creates a beam that passes through your leg. Bone is much denser, or more compact, than skin and muscle. These differences in density are captured on the X-ray film. So, when the film is developed, the bone appears white, and soft tissues, like skin and muscle, are dark grey or black. The broken part of the bone is grey.

Radiologists use other tools such as ultrasound machines and CT scanners to take pictures of the insides of our bodies. Ultrasound machines use special waves to create pictures and CT scanners use computer technology to take X-ray pictures offering many different views of our insides.

The radiologist's close-up views are pictures number one and four—a view of a brain captured by a CT scanner and an X-ray of a broken leg.

A radiologist examines some chest X-rays.

Blood Doctor

A blood doctor, or *hematologist,* often uses a light microscope to check if there is anything in our blood that could indicate diseases. He or she examines parts of the blood called *cells.* There are three main types of blood cells: red cells, white cells, and platelets. If the red cells are small, it may mean a person is not getting enough iron in his or her diet. If there are a lot of disease-fighting white blood cells, this might mean the person has an infection in his or her body.

The blood doctor's close-up view is picture number three—a view of blood cells.

AFTER YOU READ

Compare text and graphics

Look back at the notes you made about each photograph. Beside each note, add the information you learned from reading the text. Were you a careful viewer and able to gather as much information as possible from the photographs? Did the text confirm what you learned from the photographs?

Time Detectives:

Clues from Our Past

Written by Donalda Badone

READING TIP

Use clues to figure out new words

Authors often give clues in their writing to help the reader figure out the meaning of unusual or difficult words. Sometimes they give a definition or an example to explain a word. Other times the reader has to act like a detective and find out the meaning from the rest of the sentence or paragraph. As you read, jot down new words that you find.

From Labrador in the east to Vancouver in the west and from the Niagara Peninsula to Baffin Island archaeologists are at work.

Why is it important—why do archaeologists dig?

They would answer that it tells us about people who lived long ago—the Woodland First Nation people around Toronto, the Norse in Newfoundland. If we didn't carefully excavate where they left their traces, we wouldn't know anything about them. They didn't write books to tell us about their lives. It's only by investigating the things

LEARNING GOALS

You will

- read about how historians find out what happened long ago

- use clues to find the meaning of new words

they left behind that the time detectives can find out about the way they lived. That's what archaeologists do.

But doesn't everyone know that archaeology is digging up buried treasure! Finding mummies in Egypt! Breaking into old tombs for jewels and gold!

All these exciting things do sometimes happen—but only by chance. The real work of archaeology is the study of people through their physical remains, the things they used and left behind. They may never have been valuable. Most are everyday items.

Louisbourg, Nova Scotia

A small girl and boy walk along the seafront toward the Porte Dauphine. A sentry calls out in French, "Qui va là?" They give their names.

"Ah, oui. I know that name. Passez, passez," says the soldier. "Go through!"

He recognizes their last name! Does he know that their ancestor once lived here, was challenged and passed through these same gates perhaps a hundred times? Have they been travelling not only in space, from France, but also back in time to the eighteenth century? Marie-Louise and Jean walk along the path toward the spires of the town, a path they have never travelled and yet know so well.

It seems like a fairy tale that they should be returning to the place so familiar from Grandmère's stories. *Her* grandmother told of lying in bed and seeing a cannonball burst through the bedroom wall during the terrible siege. The mighty Fortress of Louisbourg looks just like it must have done in 1758 when the children's *aieux* (ancestors) had been sent back to France. They knew the town was in ruins at that time. They had come back across the ocean to see how it had risen again.

When Louisbourg was founded in 1713 on Cape Breton Island in Nova Scotia, it was the most magnificent place in North America. Travellers compared it to a French metropolis, looming strangely above the wild, uninhabited shore. "A strong and fabled city," it was said, "like some magic scene."

Legend has it that so much money was spent on the Fortress of Louisbourg that King Louis XV expected to wake up one morning in Paris and see the towers rising out of the Atlantic.

In France, medals were struck with the profile of the young king on one side and the words *Ludovicoburgum Fundatum et Munitum MDCCXX* (Louisbourg Founded and Fortified, 1720) on the reverse. Nearly 250 years later one of these was among the first artifacts dug up by archaeologists at the site.

The great fortress cost so much because almost nothing was made in Louisbourg; nearly all had to be brought in by ship. Stone and brick were imported from France. Lumber and flour came from New England. Vegetables and livestock were raised by the settlers in nearby Acadia. Coffee and sugar were brought by ship from the West Indies. Pottery and glass came from France, England, Italy, Germany, Spain, and even China.

The only item Louisbourg had for export was fish. It was to protect the cod-fishing fleet and provide a base for French trading interests in the "new" world that Louisbourg was built.

It lasted only 45 years.

During that time it was besieged, captured, and given back to the French by British forces. In 1758 it was again overcome. To put an end to the threat it posed, the British Commander-in-Chief in North America was told by his prime minister "the Fortress, together with all the works, and Defences of the Harbour, [must] be most effectually and entirely demolished."

Barrel after barrel of gunpowder was placed in 45 specially dug holes in the ground and detonated at dawn. The fort was left in ruins, its stones plundered for use elsewhere. The inhabitants, including the ancestors of Marie-Louise and Jean, were sent back to France.

The surprising fact is that the site had only a few occupants for the next 200 years. William C. MacKinnon of Sydney, Nova Scotia, wrote:

I stand on a grassy plain—I see

Nothing around that recalls to me

That city, the queen of the western sea.

There the bay's glassy waters sleep—

Here graze amid grey ruins, sheep—

Her pomp is gone, her streets are lone,

Her ramparts are with grass o'ergrown....

At the turn of this century some restoration was done but it was not until the 1920s that people began to take a real interest in Louisbourg. Parts of the site were cleared and in 1928 it was established as a National Historical Park. In 1961 the government announced plans for a reconstruction of the fortress.

Once more it was the turn of the time detectives, this time to uncover the secrets of Louisbourg—to reveal the original fortress so that its restoration would be authentic in every detail.

How did they know where to start digging? There were many good clues. On the ground, ruins of walls could still be seen. Local people had stories to tell of features and artifacts found. And, most fortunately, and most unusually, it was possible to go to France and find the 500 plans and hundreds of documents concerning the original construction.

Only the ruins of a few stone walls were left on the site of the mighty Fortress of Louisbourg when the restoration began in this century.

Archaeologists and historians pooled their knowledge with engineers and architects. Today more than 50 eighteenth-century buildings have been reconstructed and furnished to show how people lived and worked in Louisbourg. 1744 was chosen because that was the year when the fate of the fortress hung in the balance: war had been declared but Louisbourg had not yet been attacked.

Restoration archaeology has been called Humpty Dumpty archaeology—through team work, all the pieces are put back together again to provide a three-dimensional portrait of life at the time.

Because the site was so undisturbed, archaeologists at Louisbourg have one of the largest and most varied collections of eighteenth-century artifacts. It is used by other institutions when they are restoring sites of the same period. It has been said that "as many as two million wood, iron, ceramic, glass, and leather

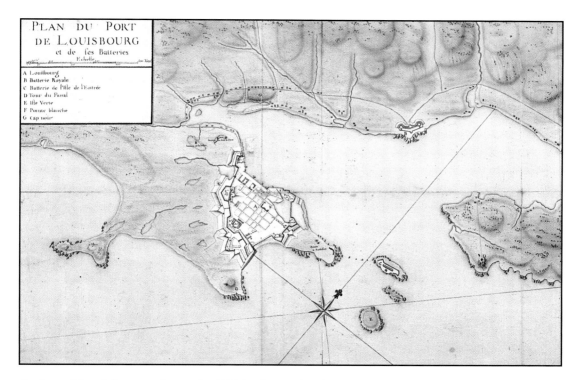

A plan of Louisbourg, drawn in 1734, shows the bastions looking out, ready to defend the town from enemies approaching from the sea.

artifacts have been unearthed at Louisbourg." This number has now been increased to five million.

Costumed interpreters go about the daily business of Louisbourg just as they would have in 1744. The site is unusually rich in historical documents—church registers of baptisms, marriages, and burials; records of legal transactions concerning property; sentences handed down by the courts; and lists of people and cargo arriving by ship.

It would not be impossible for Marie-Louise and Jean, visiting from France, to see a reconstruction of the very same house their ancestors lived in.

From the bright street, they step into the shadowy kitchen. How strange to go back in time! Before them they see great-great-great Grandmère pouring batter for thin apple-filled Breton crepes (like pancakes), while great-great-great Grandpère mends his fishing net in the corner.

Pottery for Louisbourg is made in much the same way it was in eighteenth-century France. Reproduced from pieces recovered during the excavations, and researched historically, it is used in the restored houses and inns.

Clues

Very few archaeological sites are as well documented as Louisbourg. How do archaeologists find sites to dig where there are not such good clues?

An archaeological site is any place where there is evidence of human activity. It consists of features and artifacts. Like Louisbourg it may be a place where people lived for many years or it could be a fishing camp used only in the spring. People do not need to have lived on a site; they might gather there to bury their dead or paint pictures at a sacred rock. It could be a place where stone is quarried to make tools.

Some sites are found by chance—perhaps an artifact is turned up by a plough. Most are found by archaeologists making systematic surveys.

First the archaeologist-detective will do research in libraries and archives. The lifestyle of the people tells the archaeologist what to look for. For example, if they had enemies, they would have needed to protect themselves, perhaps by building a shelter under a cliff. A village will need a source of food and water. The archaeologist looks at maps and aerial surveys and can see where sites are likely to be found.

When a general idea of where to look has been formed, a crew is gathered to walk over the ground looking for features and artifacts. A plan, or grid, is drawn up so that these clues can be located accurately. Sometimes they are marked with a red flag. Then, if the results look promising, the archaeologists will have one or more test pits dug.

When there is little to see on the ground, the archaeologist takes to the air. Many important sites have shown up in photographs taken from an airplane. Earth that has been disturbed by digging for a crop or for a building never quite returned to its original state. Aerial photography will pick up colour differences or ridges which are difficult to spot from the ground.

Life in the eighteenth century is recreated today.

More advanced and expensive methods for detecting underground disturbances include TIMS—the thermal infrared multispectral scanner which detects the temperature and energy release of different materials. A straight line revealed through this tool might indicate, for instance, a buried stone wall.

The dig site is always chosen to answer a specific question. Perhaps the people involved in reconstruction need to know where a special activity was carried on. At Louisbourg, it might be to find the place where codfish were processed.

A crew walks the field looking for traces of human activity. If an artifact or the remains of a feature are spotted, a test pit may be dug to see whether further work will uncover the site the archaeologist's research has shown to be in the area.

At another site, an archaeologist may be called in because of threatened damage to the area by construction of a road or houses. A site may be in danger from natural causes, such as floods. Even if the site itself cannot be saved, the archaeologist gains knowledge from its excavation.

AFTER YOU READ

Find the meaning of new words

Look back at the list of new words you read in this selection. Beside each word, write the meaning of the word and tell what clues you used to figure out the meaning. How will you find the meaning of any new words that did not have clues in the selection?

Eleanora's Diary:

The Journals of a Canadian Pioneer Girl

Written by Caroline Parry
Excerpted from the book Eleanora's Diary

READING TIP

Read between the lines

When reading information from journals you have to act like a detective and gather clues about the person and their life. The person writing the diary doesn't always give you all the information and you have to infer or "read between the lines" to fill in the missing information. As you read, notice how the author uses clues to find out about Eleanora's life.

Do you keep a journal, or write a diary? I do, and it's very private! Perhaps your diary is a record of where you go and what you see or do; maybe you let other people read it, or maybe not. My journal is where I write about whatever makes me glad or sad, bad-tempered or understanding. It is my own, and I don't want anyone else to read it. However, sometimes I wonder about what will happen to all my thoughts after I die. Will they stay private? If someone chanced to read my journal, say, 100 years from now, what would they think of it—and of me?

Well, recently I made friends—I guess that's the best way to describe it—with someone who kept her own journals over 150 years ago. She started when she was ten and lived in England, continued while emigrating to Canada

A photo of the Northbrook farmhouse taken in 1989. Northbrook is the home of Mrs. Norah Bastedo, a great-grand-niece of Eleanora's.

with her family, and kept writing until she was twenty-three. Those old pages bring her alive: they are a mixture of reports on what she and her family were doing, her feelings about her world, poetry, drawings, and just plain doodles.

I learned about her diaries through an archivist friend, and I first saw them at the historic family home—a big, central-Ontario farmhouse called Northbrook—where they were carefully stored in a white cardboard box. In addition, I explored an old wooden box of family papers, partially labelled and sorted. Family members through the decades had preserved all kinds of historic memorabilia, from mud bricks in the chimney to portraits of, and drawings by, my friend and her siblings. And, of course, boxes of letters and journals!

So, let me present my friend to you—or perhaps I'll let her speak for herself:

■ ■ ■

1833
This is the journal of me
ELEANORA HALLEN
who was born at Rushock in the county of Worcester
January 19, 1823

April 1st I began to keep a journal. I am ten years old.
I made Sarah and George, my brother and sister, also
Elizabeth, a cousin, April Fools; it kept me busy all morning.
We expected Miss Holmes our governess all morning, but as
it rained she did not come. I finished today the first drawing
on my card.

■ ■ ■

Many many years have passed since that rainy April Fool's Day when Eleanora began her journal. (You can think of her as living around the same time as your great-great-great-great-grandmother!) Don't you wonder why a girl of ten would happen to start a journal, one spring morning? I do—but though this article will give you the opportunity to learn many things about Eleanora, her family, and life five generations or so ago, we'll never know exactly why she started to write on this day in this year.

Eleanora's journals are full of little unknowns to puzzle over, like this one, but contain signposts8 to life in her time as well. You'll find there are many pieces of the "Eleanora puzzle" that can be put together to reveal what she and her world were like. And, sometimes, even what Eleanora does *not* say will be revealing. For now, let's start right here, with the information in this very first entry, for April 1st, 1833.

For instance, you have already learned she had at least two siblings—a brother and a sister. Does it sound to you as if her cousin were living with them as well? On to the next part of the picture: "Miss Holmes our governess." You might know already that a governess is a teacher; but you may not realize she is a special kind of private teacher who works—and usually lives—in the home of the family that employs her. (Perhaps she had been away to visit her own family on this occasion.) So guess where Eleanora went to school? At home! In fact, there was a room in her house that she refers to as the "schoolroom."

Did you also notice that one of the things Eleanora did on that April morning was

A man with a donkey, from an unsigned Hallen sketchbook dated 1833.

drawing? She and her sisters and brothers loved to draw. Finally, did you think it strange when Eleanora noted that Miss Holmes didn't come because it rained? When has the weather ever prevented you from travelling? Perhaps a blizzard or a hurricane would stop your car or plane, but not plain old rain, right?

If you know something about getting from place to place in the 1830s in the English countryside, you can figure out why rain could keep Miss Holmes away. Rural transportation was pretty limited in Eleanora's day. For

most trips, people used their own feet—or an animal's—and for longer journeys, the main form of public transportation was a horse-drawn stagecoach. Country roads weren't paved, so mud, which lasts much longer than rain, was a continual problem.

The Industrial Revolution was bringing many changes to life in England and throughout the British Empire. The invention of macadam, a kind of pressed gravel, made it easier to pave all roads, not just the ones in the cities. And canals and then railways began to spread farther and farther through the countryside. But the roads around Rushock were still just dirt tracks. The Hallens walked or rode, using donkey or horse power, almost everywhere. Every time a message was sent, a visit was made, or an errand was done, it took a great deal more arranging and effort than it takes you to lift the phone, hop on a bus or into your family van, or even pedal off on your own bike. As you read her journals, if you wonder why Eleanora writes about coming and going so much, remember how much energy it took at that time!

Now suppose you assemble the puzzle pieces to be found in Eleanora's next journal entry. You may have to read between the lines sometimes. See what fits together, and try making a list of all the ideas that occur to you as you read:

■ ■ ■

April 2nd: This day in the evening as we were sitting by the window, we saw Miss Holmes coming up the hill. I finished today a woollen ball for a baby. I put it in my mother's drawer. My father shot at a magpie and broke its leg; he tried hard to shoot it again, but could not. In the evening my father and George, when we had had tea, went to Warsley to see my aunt and uncles; it was very fine—that's why my father went out.

■ ■ ■

Here are a few connecting pieces and some more gaps to puzzle over for the April 2nd entry: how does your list compare?

—they lived on top of a hill

—some relatives lived near enough to visit—did they walk?

—maybe there was a nearby village called Warsley

—Miss Holmes was a day and a half overdue—didn't it matter? Did she send a message to say she would be late, and if so, how?

—maybe Eleanora had a baby sister or brother

—did her father shoot with a gun, or something else? (He wasn't a very good shot!) Did he hunt or shoot game birds for food?

—why was the wool in the house? For fun, or some other reason? Did they have sheep?

Well, the puzzle is getting bigger, although so are the sections that fit together. However, we still need more "edge pieces," to define the Hallen picture—these will emerge as you read on. The very next day, for instance, Eleanora explains about all her siblings.

■ ■ ■

April 3rd Today I made another wool ball for my brother Skeller Williams; he is only six years old. I think here I had better put down what our family is first; there is:

Sarah, who is 15 years,
Mary, 14 years,
George, 12 years, and a bit,
Eleanora—that's me—ten years,
Edgar, 9 years,
Preston, 7 years and a half,
Skeller Williams, six years,
Richard, three years,
Agnes, 2 years, and
Edith, 9 months, that makes ten of us.

■ ■ ■

Here's where you find out that she did have a baby sister. But that's not all—eighteen months later, in 1834, one more girl was born into the Hallen family, making a total of *eleven* children.

■ ■ ■

To go back to the wool ball I am making for Skeller Williams, I did not tell him who it was for, but said I would make him one; when I had finished it he was standing beside me, I asked him if he thought it was a pretty one and he said "yes!" so I gave it to him and he ran and showed it to my Father, Mother, and sisters.

■ ■ ■

With so many brothers and sisters, would you need friends? Young Eleanora certainly doesn't mention any in her journals. Imagine finding all your friends just within your family, from among your brothers and sisters and cousins. And Eleanora's family members were not only her friends, but her classmates, too. Think of it!

■ ■ ■

April 4th It was raining when I got up this morning, but it cleared up. I wrote my Aunt Helen and sealed up the letter. We think the pigeons have had young ones for we heard them squeak. In the evening we had just finished school, when my Aunt Chellingworth came to fetch Elizabeth home; her brother John also came—he most generally is at school.

■ ■ ■

Well, there is one little question answered—cousin Elizabeth did live with the Hallens, at least on weekdays. Cousin John must have gone to a "real" school, since he didn't stay at Rushock to study with Miss Holmes. Two other cousins lived with the Hallens most of the time. One cousin, Herbert, was a favourite, and the other, named Bella, was not—she seemed to fight with

Eleanora's sketches of herself and her brothers and sisters in 1836.

everybody! These three cousins—Elizabeth, Herbert, and Bella—are often arriving or departing in Eleanora's daily entries. So are many other relatives in her large extended family—or letters and parcels to and from them!

Do you see that you could go on piecing together the Hallen picture for a long time, just with these first few entries from Eleanora's journals to go on? She kept writing for thirteen years and filled many volumes, so there's a lot of material to think about. What's more, I discovered that transcripts of her diaries made during the 1950s, which I used initially, had been shortened or altered in many places. To understand the Hallen story fully, I returned to the originals—and this meant *more* material. So I focused on one particular year, and chose passages from surrounding years that best reveal the character of my friend and best describe her life to modern readers.

AFTER YOU READ

Think about your learning

Caroline Parry says that journals are full of "little unknown puzzles" that contain "signposts." What does she mean by this? Write at least three things you learned from this author that will help you to be a better reader by "reading between the lines."

Searching for Evidence

In this unit, you have learned how information about ourselves, our world, and places beyond our world is discovered. You have read how scientists, doctors, archaeologists, and historians use special tools, methods, and clues to find evidence. Now it is your turn to find evidence to answer a question that you have always wondered about.

▶ Before You Begin

Think of an "I wonder" question. Ask yourself these questions:

- Is my question clear and specific?
- What do I think the answer to my question is?
- How will I find evidence to answer my question?
- What do I want to know about my topic?
- What kinds of tools do the experts use to find information about my topic?
- Who will I share my information with?

"I Wonder" Questions

- I wonder how my fax machine works?
- I wonder how scientists know what dinosaurs really looked like?
- Is there life on other planets?

Michael brainstormed about the things that he has always wondered about. He selected this question.

Question: I wonder if pioneer kids played any of the same games we play?

Answer: I predict that they didn't play any of the same games that we play because they had to help around the farms so much that there was no time to play. I also think that they lived far away from one another so they couldn't play any of the team games we play today.

► Research Your Question

1 **Generate a list or web of questions about your topic.**

- Review your questions and decide which ones you will use.

Remember to focus your research on a specific "I wonder" question. If your topic is too large, you could spend all of grade six just researching the answer to that one question!

> Did they have teams and compete for prizes?
>
> Did they have special holiday games?
>
> What indoor games did they play? — PIONEER GAMES
>
> Did they have board games?
>
> Did they have seasonal games?
>
> What toys did they have and where did they get them?

Michael used a web to think about his question.

2 **Find sources of information.**

- Review the ways to search for evidence.
- Use at least three different sources of information. (At least one source must be something other than a book.)

3 **Create an organizer to record what you find out.**

- Select an organizer that will let you see the information gathered from all three sources at a glance.

Sources of Information

- the library
- the Internet
- encyclopedias
- videos
- books
- a field trip
- a person

Here is an example of an organizer you might want to use.

Did pioneer kids play the same games we do?	A Pioneer Childhood	An Internet Search	A Visit to Pioneer Village
What toys did they have?			
Did they have any organized team sports?			

▶ Your First Draft

1 **Answer your questions.**
- Work with one question at a time.
- Read each source and record what you research in your organizer.
- Record using point form and your own words.

Michael chose to use note cards to record his information. Each question has three cards, one for each source.

Source: book A Pioneer Childhood

What indoor games did

 - pinch, no smiling
 - musical chairs
 - blindman's bluff
 - word games, tongue

Source: Visit to Pioneer Village

What Indoor games did

 - buzz
 - ten fine words
 - musical chairs
 - magic lanterns

Source: Internet

What Indoor games did they play?

 - puzzles
 - musical chairs
 - me & my shadow

2 **Begin your report with a statement about your prediction.**
- Look back over the information that you found. Was your prediction correct or did the evidence make you reject it?
- Write a statement about your question, your prediction, and your conclusions.

3 **Write the body of your report.**
- Each question you collected information about should be in a separate paragraph.
- Think of interesting ways to link the information together.
- Try to vary the sentence beginnings or have a variety of sentence types.

4 **Write an ending that summarizes your report.**
- Summarize for the reader why you confirmed or rejected your prediction based on the evidence you collected.

▶ Put It All Together

You can use the information you researched in many creative ways.

- Make your information into a photo essay.
- Give a speech about your question.
- Make a bulletin board for your class or for the school.
- Gather all of the questions from the class and create a question and answer game.

Ways to Improve Your Report

- ▶ Include graphics such as diagrams, maps, or pictures if it makes your evidence clearer for the reader.
- ▶ Include some quotes from people you have interviewed or from the sources you used.
- ▶ Include a bibliography that lists all the sources you used to gather your information.

Revise and Edit

Go back and review your research report.

- Ask someone else to review your report and offer suggestions for improvements.
- Have you used complete sentences?
- Did you use connecting words to make your sentences more interesting?
- Is your spelling and grammar correct? If you are using a computer, did you use the spell check feature?
- Did you use quotation marks to indicate that you are using someone else's words?
- Is your report written or typed neatly?

Think about Your Learning

Add your own ideas to what makes a good research report.

- Did you start with an "I wonder" question?
- Did you ask questions about your topic to focus your research?
- Did you make a recording organizer?
- Did you start your report by stating your prediction and then telling if your evidence made you accept or reject your prediction?
- Was the answer to each question in a separate paragraph?
- Did you end the report by summarizing the evidence you found?

Unit 3: *Media Messages*

Advertising is part of your daily life. From the moment you get up, a jingle on the radio or an advertisement on the television is telling you what you need to make you better, faster, healthier, or smarter. Advertising is also used to try to get you to do things like vote for a particular candidate in an election or to change the way you do things such as recycling or exercising. In this unit, you will think about the different forms of advertising you experience every day. You will

- look critically at advertising in your environment
- learn about election campaigns
- examine stereotyping in advertising
- find out about how products are marketed
- read about how students your age feel about advertising
- create a product and make a plan to market it

Let's Talk Advertising

....

Written by Susan Hughes

READING TIP

Think about what you already know

Think of all the places where you see or hear advertising. Do you think that advertising was always like this? As you read, find evidence to support or reject your answer.

Did the catchy title grab you? Would it have been more appealing in flashing neon or as a speech balloon alongside a photo of your favourite actor? That's the kind of thing advertisers want to know. Advertising is all about getting your attention and making you want what the ad is selling—a product or a service—or making you want to do what the ad is suggesting, such as exercise more often or recycle.

And it isn't new. Hundreds of years ago, a farmer in the market shouted out, "Eggs for sale!" A neighbour suggested, "Try that barber." A shopkeeper's sign read: "Fresh bread." More recently, posters invited the public to stamp exhibits. Small advertisements in local newspapers suggested emigrants book their sea-passage to Canada.

Then factories began manufacturing products in large quantities. Cities grew, bringing

138

many people together. New communication technologies blossomed. With better ways to communicate more products to more consumers, there was an explosion in advertising.

It carries on today. Who hasn't seen ads for political parties, clothes, travel locations, and charities? Billboards line the highways. Radio jingles fill the airwaves. Most television channels exist only because the advertising on them pays for the programming. There are even channels dedicated to home shopping. Viewers can see

When Returning from the Theatre,
The Ball, the Evening Party, the Sleigh Drive, etc., etc.
A CUP OF HOT
OXOL
FLUID BEEF
will be found most refreshing; it will prevent you taking cold, and will ensure a good sound night's rest.
For sale by all Druggists and Grocers. Ask for OXOL and take no substitute.

NOTICE
TO
INTENDING
EMIGRANTS
FOR
NORTH AMERICA.

For Sydney, Cape Briton, Pictou, Nova Scotia, & Quebec

The Fast-Sailing, First Class, Oak-built Ship,
"SOVEREIGN,"
510 Tons Register, nearly 800 Tons Burthen.

Will be on the berth, at STROMNESS, Orkney, on the 25th July.
Intending Passengers who have made no application, will please do so with as little delay as possible.—Apply to the Owner
J. STANGER, Esq., Stromness.

INVERNESS, 15th July, 1845.

If you're in the market for a better environment, look for this mark and leave less of your own.

Choisissez ce symbole et atténuez les traces de votre présence sur la planète.

ENVIRONMENTAL CHOICE · CHOIX ENVIRONNEMENTAL

Environnement Canada   Environment Canada

Canada

GOOD YEAR

products, watch how they work, and then dial in and order them. From airborne blimps to roadside recycling boxes to the Internet, we are being bombarded with messages from advertisers.

Who produces ads? Often designers, artists, psychologists, market researchers, and copywriters work together. A successful ad is seen by many people. It can persuade even people who don't need the product that they must have it. They may buy a product because they are hoping to buy the way of life shown in the

advertisements. For example, if they buy—and then drink—a certain brand of juice they might expect to feel as if they were plunging into a cool, refreshing pool.

Advertising is a powerful tool. Its goal: to capture your attention and make you want something. Advertising has been around a long time and—it works.

AFTER YOU READ

Make a personal response

The selection ends with a statement that the goal of advertising is "to capture your attention and make you want something." Do you agree or disagree with this statement? Give your reasons.

Selling Your Sole:
How Advertising Works

Written by Monica Kulling
Illustrated by Joe Weissmann

READING TIP

Track sequence of events

Imagine that you have designed your very own new product. What do you think you would have to do to get it out for sale in the marketplace? As you read, find out the steps and the people involved in marketing a new product or idea.

Imagine you own a company that has just designed and manufactured a great new running shoe. It's comfortable. It looks terrific. It's top-of-the-line.

You know you have a winner on your hands and that your customers, once they find out about your shoe, will have a winner on their feet. Your next step is to get this message across. But how?

Advertising—that's how! Advertising will introduce your runner to the buying public. It will persuade the consumer to buy *your* runner over all the others on the market. But just *how* does advertising work, and *why*?

Once you've taken your product to an ad agency, many people get involved in the marketing campaign. Advertising agencies employ market researchers, media buyers, writers, and graphic designers. Depending on the need, they also make use of outside services, such as typesetters, photographers, and illustrators.

LEARNING GOALS

You will

- find out how a product is marketed and sold to the public
- track a sequence of events

143

Drink Milk. Love Life.

Market researchers find out who will buy your runner, what will attract this group of buyers to your runner, and what media this group of buyers regularly explores. In short, the market researcher knows consumers. If you don't already know who will "fit" your runner, a market researcher will recommend the group most likely to buy.

Once an audience for your ads has been established, a marketing strategy is developed. If this sounds a little like warfare, you're not far off the mark. Advertising works to increase product awareness, which will hopefully increase sales. It does so by exposing the buying public to their client's product often and everywhere. Advertisers will want the target group to see your runner wherever they are, whatever they're doing. The runner's unique feature is that it's cool and funky, which makes teens the most likely target group for the ad campaign. The marketing strategy will keep the teen audience in mind. The advertisers will emphasize those things that will make teens sit up and take notice. Ads that are upbeat and snappy, that use rock music, bright colours, and flashy design will probably grab the attention of the teen audience. Throw in a celebrity or two, and your runner will be off to a flying start.

At this point, the writer and the graphic designer make their contributions to the ad campaign. It's the writer's job to make up a *slogan,* or catchy phrase, to grab the attention of the target group and to write the copy that will applaud your product. It is the designer's job to create a "look" that will stick in people's minds and get them to buy the product.

Before your ads are plastered against the sky on a billboard, wedged in between videos on a rock music program or tastefully inserted in the latest issue of *Teen Culture Magazine*, you, the client, will view a presentation. The graphic designer creates full-colour layouts of the ads. These

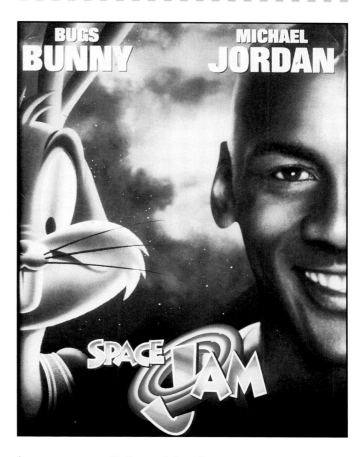

layouts are slick and look exactly the way your ad will look. If your ad campaign involves radio or television commercials, you will be presented with the script or storyboard. As the client, you have final say. If you like the approach and want to go ahead with the campaign, it's time now for the media buyers to buy advertising space.

The media buyers buy radio and TV air time,

DON'T TRASH CANS!

If everyone recycled just one more soft drink can each week for a year, we would earn thousands and thousands more dollars in "Blue Box" revenues.

Soft drink cans are made from aluminum, the most valuable material you can recycle. Recycling more cans, instead of throwing them in the garbage, would go a long way toward covering the cost of your recycling program. So when you're away from home (and your Blue Box) remember to look for the nearest recycling bin-on the street, at work, at school or take it home. Every can counts!

Don't let any get away!

CSR
CORPORATIONS
SUPPORTING
RECYCLING

where your audience spends most of its time is important if you want your ads to be seen and heard. Teens listen to rock stations. They watch TV. They travel by bus. They hang out in malls. They read music and fashion magazines. They use the Internet. If you want them to know your runner exists, your ads will have to be wherever your audience is.

Advertising will cost you money but, in the long run, it will probably make you money. The consumer may not really need those fancy new skis, that expensive designer T-shirt, or those terrific new runners, but a successful ad campaign works on the principle that people always want *more*. Graphic designer Brigitte Neukomm puts it this way: "The advertiser's job is to

magazine and newspaper ad space, billboards, busboards (advertising space on the sides of buses), ad space *inside* buses, etc. In short, anywhere you can reach your target group, and can afford to buy. Knowing

convince the buyer that it would be good to buy the advertised product. Ads create desire and consequently demand for the product or the lifestyle they're promoting."

Apart from buying and selling, advertising can also be used to educate and inform the public. We learn about a host of different services and are reminded to take care of the planet or give to certain charities. Advertising used in this way is a public service. Nine-year-old Brad Jarman of Nottawa, Ontario, made use of advertising in just this way. He wrote a radio commercial about the environment, which was aired by the local radio station. Not only did Brad write the commercial and pick out the background music for it, but he also performed it. The ad ran like this: *You can help out by composting, recycling, planting trees, and using containers for lunch instead of bags.* Kids listening to Brad's ad caught on to his idea and were soon writing their own environmental slogans.

If you've given your product a flashy, massive ad campaign, and if the campaign is followed up with more advertising, you should reap the benefits for years to come. Advertising can make the difference between a product that never really gets off the ground and one that takes off with a bang.

AFTER YOU READ

Make a flow chart

Make a flow chart like the one below that shows all the steps involved in getting a product to market.

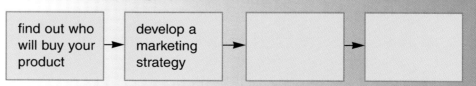

Seeing
But Not Believing

Illustrated by Tina Holdcroft

READING TIP

Set a purpose for reading

Think about a time when you wanted to buy a product or service because you saw it advertised. How did the advertisement influence you or help to make you want that service or product? As you read the next two selections, think about how you could use the information in these selections to make you a more critical viewer of advertising.

When you watch commercials on television, it always seems that the people and families in the commercials are happy, good looking, and popular. Commercials for breakfast cereal, for example, seem to show families at their best. In real life, however, getting off to school or work can be a challenging experience. The last thing you worry about is how good you look or having a friendly family conversation! The commercials seem unbelievable.

The following students were asked about the commercials they see on TV. They all felt it is wrong for commercials to promise that using a certain product will bring unrealistic results. Here are their comments.

Ashley Foster

▼

"I don't like commercials that show things that aren't real. They can't think that we believe that stuff. You know, teddy bears that get you medicine, cereal boxes that talk to you—that kind of stuff. They must think we are little kids to believe any of that. I like commercials that show the way things really are."

Pasquale Melfi

▼

"What I hate are those commercials for running shoes. You see them advertised and the person wearing them can really run. Then you buy them and guess what: you are still the same old person. You still run the way you always did—nothing's different just because you have those shoes."

Angie Dupont

▼

"Those commercials about families are so fake. The kids do something bad like spilling the pancake batter down the side of the stove and the dad just says, 'Oh, don't worry about it.' Like most parents wouldn't get mad. They never show families the way they really are."

Scottie March

▼

"I don't like commercials that show you stuff like a kid playing with an action figure, but he has a whole fort and all kinds of other accessories. Of course when you go out to buy it all you get is the one action figure. They make it seem like you are going to have so much fun, but you don't have all the stuff those kids in the commercials have."

Katie McMaster

▼

"I can't stand watching hair commercials. Like if you go and wash your hair with that shampoo, everything about your whole life changes: you are beautiful, you have lots of friends, everybody is staring at you, you go to exciting places. Get real. All you did was wash your hair."

BE A SMART
Viewer

From Zillions *magazine*

When you watch television, do you ever get frustrated because there are so many commercials? The reason the commercials are there is that they make it possible for the TV shows to appear.

Different companies purchase time with the most popular TV shows. They want to get as many people to see their products as possible. Then the advertisers can try to convince you to buy their products the next time you go to the store.

On the following pages, you will read about the different ways that advertisers influence consumers like you. You'll also meet some consumer advocates who challenged what they heard in commercials on TV.

A Tiger of an Ad

People watching sports events on TV see oodles of ads—even when it's *not* a commercial break. For example, when golfer Tiger Woods stepped onto the green at a Masters tournament, the Nike "Swoosh" logos on his shirt, sweater, and hat were visible for a full 16 and a half minutes during the broadcast.

The same amount of advertising time would have cost Nike U.S.$1,655,000 (or U.S.$100,000 per minute)!

"Sneak"-y Sell

It's not just a coincidence that new sneaker styles hit stores as kids are heading back to school. According to Mike May of the Sporting Goods Manufacturers Association, sneaker companies release their newest styles and flashiest ads at that time because they know kids want to look "cool" on the first day of school.

Tip: Older sneaker models might differ a little from the latest versions, but they'll also cost a lot less!

Kid-Testers

Have you ever tested a product you bought to make sure it lives up to what the commercial promised? Let's see what a group of student testers found when they tested two products they saw advertised on TV.

Make Your Own Gak Lab

"Attention *Gak* lovers!" bellows the TV commercial announcer.

"Now you can make your own *Gak* with the new *Make Your Own Gak Lab*. It's easy! Just pump in the water, add the secret ingredients, and in minutes, fresh, homemade *Gak!*" Our testers were eager to dig their hands into this test.

Not so fast! It took our testers 15 minutes or more to put the *Lab* together (it came unassembled), read the instructions, and mix the messy ingredients into something resembling *Gak*.

Making a mess was fun at first, but many testers agreed with David that using the *Lab* was "exhausting, and it smelled." When the kids finally produced some *Gak*, it was usually more watery than the real thing.

How much *Gak* were kids able to make? "We only made a few walnut-sized pieces," griped Dominic. "The people in the commercial were holding handfuls." Paul made a "wad" about the size of one ping-pong ball. One group of kids came up with "coloured water" and had to start from scratch a few times (using up precious ingredients) before getting any *Gak* at all. According to Lauren S.: "Kids of all ages would be misled by this ad." So the kids blasted it!

Tonka XRC Ricochet Stunt Cycle

Requires one 9 V battery and one 6 V rechargeable battery and charger (not included).

On TV, the *XRC Ricochet Stunt Cycle* drives into walls, zooms off rocks, hits the ground, and keeps going. It's "virtually unstoppable," raves the ad. Is this a remote-control dream come true? Dream, yes. Come true? Not quite.

The *Ricochet Stunt Cycle* was actually very "stoppable"—even on flat pavement, with freshly charged batteries! Each time a tester tried to operate it, another tester had to hold this top-heavy bike upright or it wouldn't budge. Once moving, it was only a matter of time before the *Ricochet* would lean to one side and grind to a halt. "It stopped every two seconds," Jennifer griped.

Our testers also drove the bike down a short staircase. ("The commercial says we're supposed to 'drive it like we hate it!'" they all yelled.) But each time it flipped and bounced down the stairs and landed at the bottom, the bike stopped moving; it had to be held upright before it could be "driven" again. "After it flips, it does *not* keep going," Sarah pointed out. Dominic said he "couldn't control it well. No one could."

Some kids, like Danny, said the commercial "does have some truth to it." But many testers agreed with Lauren S. that the ad "should not show the bike doing all the stunts a normal kid couldn't do."

Dog-gone Fad

Adorable Dalmations are facing neglect. Why? Because the popular Disney movie "101 Dalmations" sparked a Dalmation-buying frenzy. Now people are dumping the pets at animal shelters.

When people who buy pets as part of a fad grow tired of feeding and caring for them, the animals end up in shelters.

Dogs that don't get adopted are often put to sleep.

The moral: Think before you take home *any* pet. Purchasing or adopting one should be a commitment for life.

Packaging Sells

Why do toys come with so much packaging? Because the people who make toys know that packages help sell their products. Think about it: What catches your eye when you walk through a toy store? Small, modest packages, or the big, bright ones that scream out, "Buy me!"

The idea behind oversized, fancy packaging is to make you think you're getting more for your money. But what you're really getting is a toy that costs *you* more. (Who do you *think* pays for all that packaging?)

Honesty in Advertising

Adapted from the Broadcast Code for Advertising for Children
Illustrated by Kathryn Adams

People who advertise on television to children under 12 years of age have to follow rules.

- The product demonstrated on TV must look and perform the same way when you buy it and bring it home.
- If you buy a model or a craft kit, the instructions should be easy to follow.
- The price of the product must be clear. If you have to buy batteries separately, it must be clearly stated.
- If toys shown together are sold separately, this must be made clear.

AFTER YOU READ

Be a critical viewer

Think of how you viewed and listened to advertising before you read these selections. Make a list of the techniques that advertisers use to try to influence consumers. How will knowing this information help you when you see products and services advertised?

THE LAST-PLACE
SPORTS POEMS
of Jeremy Bloom

Written by Gordon Korman and Bernice Korman
Illustrated by Jane Kurisu and Harvey Chan

READING TIP

Listen for the rhyme scheme

One of the techniques that poets use to make their poems pleasing to the reader's ear is to use rhyming words. When these rhyming words follow the same pattern throughout the poem, it is called a rhyming scheme. As you read the two poems, listen to see if both poems use the same rhyme scheme.

Jeremy is in poetry class again and doesn't know what to write about. Then his two best friends appear, full of excitement about their sports teams. Jeremy's teacher suggests that he write about sports. Here are two of the poems he wrote.

The Super Bowl

The Super Bowl—it's Super-great!
But watch that you don't suffocate
In Super-hoopla, Super-hype,
As broadcasters spew Super-tripe

Of Super-teams we're here to see
Play Super-offense, Super-D,
And dish out Super-hits and hurts,
While Super-stores sell Super-shirts,

And Super-hot dogs, Super-drinks,
Who cares if the *game* always stinks?
They come in airplanes, cars, and
    trucks,
Those Super-seats cost Super-bucks!

Not counting souvenirs you trash
Upon returning from this bash.
A Super-costly Super-trip—
Your Super-team lost forty-zip!

LEARNING GOALS

You will

- read poems about how sports
  events and sports stars are used to
  sell products

- compare rhyming schemes used in
  two poems

161

GONE Commercial

I'm gonna be a superstar;
    of that I have no doubt,
But I will not be known for all
    the batters I strike out,
Or power plays, or touchdowns, or
    my brutal slam-dunk force,
My super-fame will come from all
    the products I endorse.

From underwear, to limousines,
    to matzo balls by Herschel,
I'll be the guy to catch your eye,
    the star of each commercial.
My famous face will do the job
    far more than words could tell.
They won't say, "Man, can that guy play!"
    they'll say, "Man, can he sell!"

On billboards pushing toothpaste,
    and on every tuna tin,
No oatmeal box is printed
    without my infectious grin.
My voice is on the radio,
    my face is on TV—
You wouldn't buy a paper clip
    unless it came from me!

So though I'm not that good at sports,
    I'll make it just the same.
Some day my face will hang in the
    Endorsement Hall of Fame.

AFTER YOU READ

Write a poem using a rhyme scheme

Brainstorm a list of words describing your favourite sporting event. Beside each word, try to think of a rhyming word. Use these words to create your own poem about advertising and sports events. Use a rhyme scheme like one of those used in the poems you just read or create your own rhyme scheme.

Elections and Advertising

Written by Linda Granfield
Illustrated by Scot Ritchie

READING TIP

Use context clues to figure out new words

As you read, you might find words that you do not know. Sometimes the author helps you to understand those words by giving you a definition or an explanation. Sometimes you have to figure out the meaning from the rest of the sentence or paragraph. Jot down any new words you find as you read this selection.

Once a federal election has been called and an election day is set, the countdown begins.

There is a minimum of 36 days before people vote and there's plenty to be done. Election day is called "Day 0" and "Day 21" is Nomination Day. On that day, a list with the names of every candidate in Canada is drawn up.

How do candidates get nominated?

Any person who is a qualified voter can run for office. The candidate may seek election in only one electoral district at a time.

A candidate who wants to represent a political party must win the support of that party: this is usually done at a nomination meeting held by party members in the electoral district. A candidate who is not endorsed by a party can run as an independent candidate. But that's only the beginning.

Let's say Tiffany Lampe wants to be an MP for the Edisonville district. She must have an official agent (who handles all the financial transactions of the campaign) and an auditor (someone who will check financial reports). The returning officer in the district will give Tiffany official nomination papers. To be nominated officially, she needs at least 100 signatures of voters who live in the Edisonville district. All Tiffany's nomination papers must be completed and turned in by 2 p.m. on Day 21. She also needs to make a money deposit to show she's serious about running for office.

LEARNING GOALS

You will

- find out how election candidates use marketing and advertising techniques to persuade people to vote for them

- use context clues to figure out the meaning of new words

At the end of Day 21, if Tiffany is the only candidate, the returning officer will close the election and declare her the winner by *acclamation*.

It was easy for Tiffany, wasn't it? For most candidates there's a great deal more work.

Let's say two other people decide to run against Tiffany Lampe. She'll have to campaign to win voters' support. She'll choose a *campaign manager* to oversee every detail of her campaign. Tiffany will need someone who has a lot of campaign experience. The manager will see that a headquarters is set up, maybe in a vacant store. He or she will make sure Tiffany gets to the opening of that new seniors' centre and that she has her picture taken kissing a cute baby. It's important for Tiffany to be known by voters. The manager will also arrange fundraising dinners so the money will keep coming in and will hire speech-writers to help Tiffany present her ideas well to the voters.

Campaigning is hard work. Tiffany will have to go *mainstreeting:* she'll stroll through shopping malls or down busy streets in her area, shaking hands and chatting with voters. She wants to get to know the voters and let them get to know her. What are their concerns? How can she help them?

By the time Tiffany Lampe is elected, she may have gained five kilograms from too much fast food and too many benefit dinner banquets. She may have dark circles under her eyes from lack of sleep after late-night speeches. And her family may hardly recognize her because she's hardly been home. But it's all part of a candidate's life and Tiffany Lampe hopes that on election day her efforts will result in victory.

"Getting to Know You...."

When Tiffany Lampe announced her candidacy in your riding, maybe you'd never heard of her before. Why should you give her your vote?

Slogans

When you urge your school team on to victory at the hockey playoffs, you cheer, "Go get 'em, Rivercrest!" or whatever your school is called. This slogan whips up team spirit. Election slogans work the same way. Long ago, slogans were the battle cries of warriors; now slogans appear on election posters, television commercials, and buttons.

Here are some slogans from past elections:

Notice that the name of the candidate is usually part of the slogan. Some candidates today hire advertising agencies to create election slogans that will keep their names in the voters' minds right until election day.

She's just a name to you. How can you get more information about her?

Choosing a candidate can be difficult. Candidates from different political parties often say basically the same thing. After all, no candidate is going to say he or she doesn't care about acid rain. Listen carefully. Tiffany may propose a quick solution. Mr. C. may say acid rain is not a top priority issue; the budget is his concern.

How do you find out what Tiffany and the other candidates stand for? Campaign literature is one guide. Political parties and candidates print tons of brochures. Usually these feature biographies of the candidates and outline key election topics.

Local and national newspapers are filled with articles and editorials about candidates and what they think. And television can let you see some parliamentarians in action. If Mr. C. is running for reelection, you may want to see how he performs daily in Ottawa, on TV.

You can also talk to Tiffany face to face. Candidates visit neighbourhoods to talk to the voters. Tiffany may knock on your door or attend a community picnic. That's your chance to ask her what she really feels about issues of concern to you.

"How Do I Look?"

When you go to apply for a job at the hardware store, you don't spray your hair green and wear a ripped T-shirt—and expect to get the job. You dress for success.

First impressions are important in elections, too, and candidates spend lots of time and money "improving their images" before meeting voters.

Television brings candidates into voters' living rooms. Candidates who "look bad" on TV hire media experts to groom them for on-screen appearances. Some candidates get complete make-overs, everything from a new hairdo and contact lenses to a snappier wardrobe.

Political parties produce television commercials that are broadcast during the last four weeks before election day. But such advertising is banned the day before election day—and on the day itself.

Some candidates have trademarks—certain items that become identified with them. Prime Minister Lester Pearson

wore bow ties and Prime Minister Pierre Trudeau often sported a rose in his lapel. These trademarks help politicians set themselves apart from the rest of the pack and give you something to remember.

AFTER YOU READ

Find the meaning of new words

Look back at your list of new words. Beside each new word, write the meaning of the word and tell what clues you used to figure out the meaning of the word.

The Doughnuts

Written and illustrated by Robert McCloskey

One Friday night in November Homer overheard his mother talking on the telephone to Aunt Agnes over in Centerburg. "I'll stop by with the car in about half an hour and we can go to the meeting together," she said, because tonight was the night the Ladies' Club was meeting to discuss plans for a box social and to knit and sew for the Red Cross.

"I think I'll come along and keep Uncle Ulysses company while you and Aunt Agnes are at the meeting," said Homer.

So after Homer had combed his hair and his mother had looked to see if she had her knitting instructions and the right size needles, they started for town.

Homer's Uncle Ulysses and Aunt Agnes have a very up and coming lunch room over in Centerburg, just across from the court house on the town square. Uncle Ulysses is a man with advanced ideas and a weakness for labor saving devices. He equipped the lunch room with automatic toasters,

LEARNING GOALS

You will

- read a humorous story about how advertising helped to solve a problem

- find out how the language used by story characters can give clues to the reader about when the story takes place

171

automatic coffee maker, automatic dish washer, and an automatic doughnut maker. All just the latest thing in labor saving devices. Aunt Agnes would throw up her hands and sigh every time Uncle Ulysses bought a new labor saving device. Sometimes she became unkindly disposed toward him for days and days. She was of the opinion that Uncle Ulysses just frittered away his spare time over at the barber shop with the sheriff and the boys, so, what was the good of a labor saving device that gave you more time to fritter?

When Homer and his mother got to Centerburg they stopped at the lunch room, and after Aunt Agnes had come out and said, "My, how that boy does grow!" which was what she always said, she went off with Homer's mother in the car. Homer went into the lunch room and said, "Howdy, Uncle Ulysses!"

"Oh, hello, Homer. You're just in time," said Uncle Ulysses. "I've been going over this automatic doughnut machine, oiling the machinery and cleaning the works ... wonderful things, these labor saving devices."

"Yep," agreed Homer, and he picked up a cloth and started polishing the metal trimmings while Uncle Ulysses tinkered with the inside workings.

"Opfwo-oof!!" sighed Uncle Ulysses and, "Look here, Homer, you've got a mechanical mind. See if you can find where these two pieces fit in. I'm going across to the barber shop for a spell, 'cause there's somethin' I've got to talk to the sheriff about. There won't be much business here until the double feature is over and I'll be back before then."

Then as Uncle Ulysses went out the door he said, "Uh, Homer, after you get the pieces in place, would you mind mixing up a batch of doughnut batter and putting it in the machine? You could turn the switch and make a few doughnuts to have on hand for the crowd after the movie ... if you don't mind."

"O.K.," said Homer, "I'll take care of everything."

A few minutes later a customer came in and said, "Good evening, Bud."

Homer looked up from putting the last piece in the doughnut machine and said, "Good evening, Sir, what can I do for you?"

"Well, young feller, I'd like a cup o' coffee and some doughnuts," said the customer.

"I'm sorry, Mister, but we won't have any doughnuts for about half an hour, until I can mix some dough and start this machine. I could give you some very fine sugar rolls instead."

"Well, Bud, I'm in no real hurry so I'll just have a cup o' coffee and wait around a bit for the doughnuts. Fresh doughnuts are always worth waiting for is what I always say."

"O.K.," said Homer, and he drew a cup of coffee from Uncle Ulysses' super automatic coffee maker.

"Nice place you've got here," said the customer.

"Oh, yes," replied Homer, "this is a very up and coming lunch room with all the latest improvements."

"Yes," said the stranger, "must be a good business. I'm in business too. A traveling man in outdoor advertising. I'm a sandwich man, Mr. Gabby's my name."

"My name is Homer. I'm glad to meet you, Mr. Gabby. It must be a fine profession, traveling and advertising sandwiches."

"Oh, no," said Mr. Gabby, "I don't advertise sandwiches, I just wear any kind of an ad, one sign on front and one sign on behind, this way.... Like a sandwich. Ya know what I mean?"

"Oh, I see. That must be fun, and you travel too?" asked Homer as he got out the flour and the baking powder.

"Yeah, I ride the rods between jobs, on freight trains, ya know what I mean?"

"Yes, but isn't that dangerous?" asked Homer.

"Of course there's a certain amount a risk, but you take any method a travel these days, it's all dangerous. Ya know what I mean? Now take airplanes for instance...."

Just then a large shiny black car stopped in front of the lunch room and a chauffeur helped a lady out of the rear door. They both came inside and the lady smiled at Homer and said, "We've stopped for a light snack. Some doughnuts and coffee would be simply marvelous."

Then Homer said, "I'm sorry, Ma'm, but the doughnuts won't be ready until I make this batter and start Uncle Ulysses' doughnut machine."

"Well now aren't *you* a clever young man to know how to make *doughnuts!*"

"Well," blushed Homer, "I've really never done it before but I've got a receipt to follow."

"Now, young man, you simply must allow me to help. You know, I haven't made doughnuts for years, but I know the best receipt for doughnuts. It's marvelous, and we really must use it."

"But, Ma'm...." said Homer.

"Now just *wait* till you taste these doughnuts," said the lady. "Do you have an apron?" she asked as she took off her fur coat and her rings and her jewelry and rolled up her sleeves. "Charles," she said to the chauffeur, "hand me that baking powder, that's right, and, young man, we'll need some nutmeg."

So Homer and the chauffeur stood by and handed things and cracked the eggs while the lady mixed and stirred. Mr. Gabby sat on his stool, sipped his coffee, and looked on with great interest.

"There!" said the lady when all of the ingredients were mixed. "Just *wait* till you taste these doughnuts!"

"It looks like an awful lot of batter," said Homer as he stood on a chair and poured it into the doughnut machine with the help of the chauffeur. "It's about *ten* times as much as Uncle Ulysses ever makes."

"But wait till you taste them!" said the lady with an eager look and a smile.

Homer got down from the chair and pushed a button on the machine marked *"Start."* Rings of batter started dropping into the hot fat. After a ring of batter was cooked on one side, an automatic gadget turned it over and the other side would cook. Then another automatic gadget gave the doughnut a little push and it rolled neatly down a little chute, all ready to eat.

"That's a simply *fascinating* machine," said the lady as she waited for the first doughnut to roll out.

"Here, young man, *you* must have the first one. Now isn't that just *too* delicious!? Isn't it simply marvelous?"

"Yes, Ma'm, it's very good," replied Homer as the lady handed doughnuts to Charles and to Mr. Gabby and asked if they didn't think they were simply divine doughnuts.

"It's an old family receipt!" said the lady with pride.

Homer poured some coffee for the lady and her chauffeur and for Mr. Gabby, and a glass of milk for himself. Then they all sat down at the lunch counter to enjoy another few doughnuts apiece.

"I'm so glad you enjoy my doughnuts," said the lady. "But now, Charles, we really must be going. If you will just take this apron, Homer, and put two dozen doughnuts in a bag to take along, we'll be on our way. And, Charles, don't forget to pay the young man." She rolled down her sleeves and put on her jewelry, then Charles managed to get her into her big fur coat.

"Good night, young man, I haven't had so much fun in years. I *really* haven't!" said the lady as she went out the door and into the big shiny car.

"Those are sure good doughnuts," said Mr. Gabby as the car moved off.

"You bet!" said Homer. Then he and Mr. Gabby stood and watched the automatic doughnut machine make doughnuts.

After a few dozen more doughnuts had rolled down the little chute, Homer said, "I guess that's about enough doughnuts to sell to the after theater customers. I'd better turn the machine off for a while."

Homer pushed the button marked *"Stop"* and there was a little click, but nothing happened. The rings of batter kept right on dropping into the hot fat, and an automatic gadget kept right on turning them over, and another automatic gadget kept right on giving them a little push, and the doughnuts kept right on rolling down the little chute, all ready to eat.

"That's funny," said Homer, "I'm sure that's the right button!" He pushed it again but the automatic doughnut maker kept right on making doughnuts.

"Well I guess I must have put one of those pieces in backwards," said Homer.

"Then it might stop if you pushed the button marked *'Start,'"* said Mr. Gabby.

Homer did, and the doughnuts still kept rolling down the little chute, just as regular as a clock can tick.

"I guess we could sell a few more doughnuts," said
Homer, "but I'd better telephone Uncle Ulysses over at the
barber shop." Homer gave the number and while he waited
for someone to answer, he counted thirty-seven doughnuts
roll down the little chute.

Finally someone answered, "Hello! This is the sarber
bhop, I mean the barber shop."

"Oh, hello, sheriff. This is Homer. Could I speak to
Uncle Ulysses?"

"Well, he's playing pinochle right now," said the sheriff.
"Anythin' I can tell 'im?"

"Yes," said Homer. "I pushed the button marked
Stop on the doughnut machine but the rings of batter

keep right on dropping into the hot fat, and an automatic gadget keeps right on turning them over, and another automatic gadget keeps giving them a little push, and the doughnuts keep right on rolling down the little chute! It won't stop!"

"O.K. Wold the hire, I mean, hold the wire and I'll tell 'im." Then Homer looked over his shoulder and counted another twenty-one doughnuts roll down the little chute, all ready to eat. Then the sheriff said, "He'll be right over.... Just gotta finish this hand."

"That's good," said Homer. "G'by, sheriff."

The window was full of doughnuts by now so Homer and Mr. Gabby had to hustle around and start stacking them on plates and trays and lining them up on the counter.

"Sure are a lot of doughnuts!" said Homer.

"You bet!" said Mr. Gabby. "I lost count at twelve hundred and two and that was quite a while back."

People had begun to gather outside the lunch room window, and someone was saying, "There are almost as many doughnuts as there are people in Centerburg, and I wonder how in tarnation Ulysses thinks he can sell all of 'em!"

Every once in a while somebody would come inside and buy some, but while somebody bought two to eat and a dozen to take home, the machine made three dozen more.

By the time Uncle Ulysses and the sheriff arrived and pushed through the crowd, the lunch room was a calamity of doughnuts! Doughnuts in the window, doughnuts piled high on the shelves, doughnuts stacked on plates, doughnuts lined up twelve deep all along the counter, and doughnuts still rolling down the little chute, just as regular as a clock can tick.

"Hello, sheriff, hello, Uncle Ulysses, we're having a little trouble here," said Homer.

"Well, I'll be dunked!!" said Uncle Ulysses.

"Derned ef you won't be when Aggy gits home," said the sheriff.

"Mighty fine doughnuts though. What'll you do with 'em all, Ulysses?" said the sheriff.

Uncle Ulysses groaned and said, "What will Aggy say? We'll never sell 'em all."

Then Mr. Gabby, who hadn't said anything for a long time, stopped piling doughnuts and said, "What you need is an advertising man. Ya know what I mean? You got the doughnuts, ya gotta create a market.... Understand?... It's balancing the demand with the supply.... That sort of thing."

"Yep!" said Homer. "Mr. Gabby's right. We have to enlarge our market. He's an advertising sandwich man, so if we hire him, he can walk up and down in front of the theater and get the customers."

"You're hired, Mr. Gabby!" said Uncle Ulysses.

Then everybody pitched in to paint the signs and to get Mr. Gabby sandwiched between. They painted "SALE ON DOUGHNUTS" in big letters on the window too.

Meanwhile the rings of batter kept right on dropping into the hot fat, and an automatic gadget kept right on turning them over, and another automatic gadget kept right on giving them a little push, and the doughnuts kept right on rolling down the little chute, just as regular as a clock can tick.

"I certainly hope this advertising works," said Uncle Ulysses, wagging his head. "Aggy'll certainly throw a fit if it don't."

The sheriff went outside to keep order, because there was quite a crowd by now—all looking at the doughnuts and guessing how many thousand there were, and watching new ones roll down the little chute, just as regular as a clock can tick. Homer and Uncle Ulysses kept stacking doughnuts. Once in a while somebody bought a few, but not very often.

Then Mr. Gabby came back and said, "Say, you know there's not much use o' me advertisin' at the theater. The show's all over, and besides almost everybody in town is out front watching that machine make doughnuts!"

"Zeus!" said Uncle Ulysses. "We must get rid of these doughnuts before Aggy gets here!"

"Looks like you will have ta hire a truck ta waul 'em ahay, I mean haul 'em away!!" said the sheriff who had just come in. Just then there was a noise and a shoving out front and the lady from the shiny black car and her chauffeur came pushing through the crowd and into the lunch room.

"Oh, gracious!" she gasped, ignoring the doughnuts, "I've lost my diamond bracelet, and I know I left it here on the counter," she said, pointing to a place where the doughnuts were piled in stacks of two dozen.

"Yes, Ma'm, I guess you forgot it when you helped make the batter," said Homer.

Then they moved all the doughnuts around and looked for the diamond bracelet, but they couldn't find it anywhere. Meanwhile the doughnuts kept rolling down the little chute, just as regular as a clock can tick.

After they had looked all around the sheriff cast a suspicious eye on Mr. Gabby, but Homer said, "He's all right, sheriff, he didn't take it. He's a friend of mine."

Then the lady said, "I'll offer a reward of one hundred dollars for that bracelet! It really *must* be found ... it *really* must!"

"Now don't you worry, lady," said the sheriff. "I'll get your bracelet back!"

"Zeus! This is terrible!" said Uncle Ulysses. "First all of these doughnuts and then on top of all that, a lost diamond bracelet...."

Mr. Gabby tried to comfort him, and he said, "There's always a bright side. That machine'll probably run outta batter in an hour or two."

If Mr. Gabby hadn't been quick on his feet Uncle Ulysses would have knocked him down, sure as fate.

Then while the lady wrung her hands and said, "We must find it, we *must!*" and Uncle Ulysses was moaning about what Aunt Agnes would say, and the sheriff was eyeing Mr. Gabby, Homer sat down and thought hard.

Before twenty more doughnuts could roll down the little chute he shouted, "SAY! I know where the bracelet is! It was lying here on the counter and got mixed up in the batter by mistake! The bracelet is cooked inside one of these doughnuts!"

"Why ... I really believe you're right," said the lady through her tears. "Isn't that *amazing?* Simply *amazing!*"

"I'll be durn'd!" said the sheriff.

FRESH DOUGHNUTS
2 FOR 5¢
WHILE THEY LAST
$100.00 PRIZE
FOR FINDING
A BRACELET
INSIDE A DOUGHNUT
P.S. YOU HAVE TO GIVE THE
BRACELET BACK

"OhH-h!" moaned Uncle Ulysses. "Now we have to break up all of these doughnuts to find it. Think of the *pieces!* Think of the *crumbs!* Think of what *Aggy* will say!"

"Nope," said Homer. "We won't have to break them up. I've got a plan."

So Homer and the advertising man took some cardboard and some paint and printed another sign. They put this sign in the window, and the sandwich man wore two more signs that said the same thing and walked around in the crowd out front.

THEN ... The doughnuts began to sell! *Everybody* wanted to buy doughnuts, *dozens* of doughnuts!

And that's not all. Everybody bought coffee to dunk the doughnuts in too. Those that didn't buy coffee bought milk or soda. It kept Homer and the lady and the chauffeur and Uncle Ulysses and the sheriff busy waiting on the people who wanted to buy doughnuts.

When all but the last couple of hundred doughnuts had been sold, Rupert Black shouted, "I GAWT IT!!" and sure enough ... there was the diamond bracelet inside of his doughnut!

Then Rupert went home with a hundred dollars, the citizens of Centerburg went home full of doughnuts, the lady and her chauffeur drove off with the diamond bracelet, and Homer went home with his mother when she stopped by with Aunt Aggy.

As Homer went out of the door he heard Mr. Gabby say, "Neatest trick of merchandising I ever seen," and Aunt Aggy was looking sceptical while Uncle Ulysses was saying, "The rings of batter kept right on dropping into the hot fat, and the automatic gadget kept right on turning them over, and the other automatic gadget kept right on giving them a little push, and the doughnuts kept right on rolling down the little chute just as regular as a clock can tick—they just kept right on a comin', an' a comin', an' a comin', an' a comin'."

AFTER YOU READ

Use modern language and expressions

Write down a list of the words or expressions that helped you to identify the time period when this story might have taken place. If you wanted to change the story to take place today, how would you change these words or expressions?

Buy BJ's Cola

Media Messages

In this unit, you have read about how advertisers try to persuade people to buy products or ideas. You have discovered that a great deal of planning goes into selling a product or idea and that many people are involved. Now it is your turn to create a new product and develop an advertising plan to sell your product to others.

▶ Before You Begin

You could also choose an existing product that includes new features.

Think about a new product to advertise. Ask yourself these questions:

- What will my product look like?
- Who will want to buy my product?
- How will I persuade them to buy my product?
- What advertising techniques will I use?
- Where will I advertise?

Dean created a "thinking" chart to help him decide what product to advertise.

Advertising Techniques

- slogan
- logo
- jingle
- visual
- celebrity endorsement
- research facts

POPULAR ITEMS	FEATURES	MY PRODUCT
Running Shoes	Logos, Comfort	Tear-Away Running Shoes
Baseball Hats	Sports Teams	
Track Suits	Tear-Aways	
Video Games	Monsters, Graphics	
Music CD's	Popular Songs, Bands	

▶ Create Your Product

1 **Choose your product.**
- Draw a rough sketch of your product.
- Jot down the special features.
- Think of ways it will be appealing to possible buyers.

This is a rough sketch of Dean's tear-away running shoes.

2 **Develop an advertising strategy.**
- Review the steps involved in selling a product.
- Make a plan that includes the following information: the market or consumer group that will buy the product and where and how you will advertise.

Dean decided to use a chart to organize his marketing information.

Choose a Strategy

▶ If you plan to advertise on the radio, you might want to use a catchy jingle.

▶ If you plan to advertise on TV, you might need a TV script for your actors to follow.

Magazine Radio
Billboard **TV**

Delgada Shoes

Who is the target group?	My shoe is for ages 10 – Adult.
Where will I advertise this product?	I will advertise in newspapers, on radio, and on billboards.
Do I need a script for TV or radio?	Yes, I will need a script for a radio commercial.
Where will I advertise as a follow-up to the initial advertising?	I will first use a radio commercial to get attention and then follow up with a TV advertisement.
What will my slogan be?	My slogan is: Run Faster, Jump Higher, Play Harder.

The **Market** for a product is the consumer group most likely to buy the product—seniors or teenagers, for example.

▶ Your First Draft

1 **Create your written advertisement.**
- Think about advertisements that use written words.
- What features do they have in common?
- Make a list of the words you want to use to advertise your product.

Here is Dean's written advertisement.

> # Run Faster,
> # Jump Higher,
> # Play Harder.

> **Remember,** the words you choose must be so powerful that your audience will remember them even if they only see or hear those words for a few seconds.

2 **Add a visual (photo or illustration) to your advertisement.**
- Decide how you are going to represent your product. Will you use a close-up? show someone using it?

This is how Dean decided to visually represent his product.

Other Ways to Advertise

Create additional ads that could be used on the radio and on TV. How will those ads be different from what you created here?

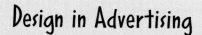

▶ Put It All Together

When your advertisement is finished, you can post it on the bulletin board or make a classroom collection of products and ads in a magazine format.

Design in Advertising

The design of your advertisement is very important. Choose the look and size of lettering that best represents your product.

Type

Revise and Edit

Go back and look at your advertisement.

- Ask some classmates to look at your work. Listen to their suggestions. Are there any improvements that you could make?
- Did you emphasize the important text features of your advertisement by using different typefaces (e.g., boldface)?
- Did you create eye-catching visuals?
- Proofread your work for errors in spelling, punctuation, and grammar.

Think about Your Learning

Add your own ideas about what makes a good advertising and marketing plan.

- Have you identified your target market?
- Is your product something that others will want or need?
- Have you identified the best way to reach your target?
- Did you select advertising techniques that would appeal to your market?
- Did you create advertisements that people could read quickly?

ACKNOWLEDGMENTS

Permission to reprint copyrighted material is gratefully acknowledged. Every effort has been made to trace ownership of all copyrighted material and to secure permission from copyright holders. In the event of any question arising as to the use of any material, we will be pleased to make the necessary corrections in future printings.

Photographs
p. 6 © Stan Behal/Toronto Sun; p. 7 (left) courtesy of Paquin Entertainment Group, (middle) Lydia Pawlak/National Ballet of Canada, (right) © Norm Betts/Toronto Sun; p. 8 (top) Canadian Sport Images; p. 9 (top left) National Space Agency, (top right) Toronto Sun, (bottom left) Canadian Sport Images, (bottom right) CBC/Robin Johnston; p. 11 courtesy of Carlee and Christy Panylyk; p. 12 courtesy of Heather Kao; p. 13 © Randy Velocci/The Globe & Mail; p. 14 courtesy of Penny Olson; p. 15 courtesy of Kevin Stonefield/Georgetown Elementary School; p. 16 courtesy of Iris Bonaise; p. 43 The Rick Hansen Institute/Roger Gould/Nike International; p. 44 Toronto Sun; pp. 45-47 courtesy of The Rick Hansen Institute; p. 78 (top) © PhotoDisc, (bottom left) courtesy of NASA, (bottom right) © PhotoDisc; p. 79 (top left) © Corel Corporation, (top middle, right) © PhotoDisc, (middle) © 1996 Image Club Graphics—Objectgear vol. 10, (bottom) Royal Tyrrell Museum/Alberta Community Development; pp. 85, 88, 90 courtesy of NASA; p. 104 (top) Visuals Unlimited/© K. G. Murti, (middle) Visuals Unlimited/© David M. Phillips, (bottom) Visuals Unlimited/© Cabisco; p. 105 (top) Dwight Brown, (bottom) © Larry Gatz/Image Bank; p. 106 (top) Dwight Brown, (bottom) © PhotoDisc; p. 107 (top right) Visuals Unlimited/© Jeffrey Howe, (bottom right) Visuals Unlimited/© Michael G. Gabridge, (top left) Visuals Unlimited/ © K. G. Murti, (bottom left) Visuals Unlimited/© S. Flegler; p. 108 Dwight Brown; p. 109 (top left) © Visuals Unlimited, (top right) Visuals Unlimited/© A. L. Blum, (middle left) Visuals Unlimited/© David M. Phillips, (middle right) © 1991 Scott Camazine, (bottom) Visuals Unlimited © SIU; p. 110 © Steve Dunwell/Image Bank; p. 111 Dwight Brown; pp. 112-113 Royal Tyrrell Museum/Alberta Community Development; p. 114 from Nelson archives; p. 118 Parks Canada, Fortress of Louisbourg (DS 98-469); p. 119 Parks Canada, Fortress of Louisbourg; p. 120 (top) Parks Canada, Fortress of Louisbourg (DS 95-353), (bottom) Parks Canada, Fortress of Louisbourg (DS 98-474); p. 122 (left) Parks Canada, Fortress of Louisbourg (DS 98-471), (right) Parks Canada, Fortress of Louisbourg (DS 98-472); p. 123 Metropolitan Toronto and Region Conservation Authority/Bob Burgar; p. 125 courtesy of Caroline Parry; p. 139 (top) courtesy Glenbow Museum (NA-3909-1), (bottom) Scala/Art Resource, New York (JM1533); p. 140 (top) courtesy of Environmental Choice Program, (bottom) © Corel Corporation; p. 141 (left) © Corel Corporation, (right) © Al Harvey; p. 144 courtesy of the Dairy Farmers of Ontario, p. 145 © Photofest; p. 146 courtesy of CSR: Corporations Supporting Recycling; p. 155 (top) © Canapress, (bottom) Dave Starrett; pp. 156-157 © Richard Hutchings; p. 158 (top) © Gary Gay/Image Bank, (bottom) © Richard Hutchings

Illustrations
Cover: (top) Todd Ryoji, (bottom) Heather Holbrook; pp. 6-7 Steve MacEachern; pp. 10-17 Farida Zaman; pp. 19, 21, 22-25 Tadeusz Majewski; pp. 27-28, 30-31 Karen Reczuch; pp. 32-37, 39, 41 Kevin O'Malley; pp. 48-49 Tina Holdcroft; p. 50 Shel Silverstein; p. 51 Scott Medlock; p. 52 Leon Zernitsky; pp. 54-55, 57-58, 60-62 Geoff Butler; pp. 65-69, 71-72 Birgitta Säflund; pp. 74-77 Jun Park; pp. 78-79 Dave McKay; pp. 81, 83 Jean-Pierre Normand; pp. 84-87, 89 Bart Vallecoccia; pp. 93, 95, 97, 99, 101-102 Kim LaFave; pp. 115-116 Joe Morse; pp. 132-135 Jun Park; pp. 136-137 Steve Attoe; pp. 142-143 Joe Weissmann; pp. 149-153 Tina Holdcroft; p. 159 Kathryn Adams; p. 161 Jane Kurisu; p. 162 Harvey Chan; pp. 165-169 Scot Ritchie; pp. 171, 173, 175, 178, 179, 181, 183, 184 Robert McCloskey; pp. 186-189 Jun Park

Text
"It's Easy to Dream" from MUD, MOON AND ME by Zaro Weil. Text copyright © 1989 by Zaro Weil. Reprinted by permission of Houghton Mifflin Co. All rights reserved. "The Night of the